Independent Task Force Report No. 76

The Work Ahead

*Machines, Skills, and U.S. Leadership
in the Twenty-First Century*

John Engler and Penny Pritzker, *Chairs*
Edward Alden, *Project Director*
Laura Taylor-Kale, *Deputy Project Director*

The Council on Foreign Relations (CFR) is an independent, nonpartisan membership organization, think tank, and publisher dedicated to being a resource for its members, government officials, business executives, journalists, educators and students, civic and religious leaders, and other interested citizens in order to help them better understand the world and the foreign policy choices facing the United States and other countries. Founded in 1921, CFR carries out its mission by maintaining a diverse membership, with special programs to promote interest and develop expertise in the next generation of foreign policy leaders; convening meetings at its headquarters in New York and in Washington, DC, and other cities where senior government officials, members of Congress, global leaders, and prominent thinkers come together with Council members to discuss and debate major international issues; supporting a Studies Program that fosters independent research, enabling CFR scholars to produce articles, reports, and books and hold roundtables that analyze foreign policy issues and make concrete policy recommendations; publishing *Foreign Affairs*, the preeminent journal on international affairs and U.S. foreign policy; sponsoring Independent Task Forces that produce reports with both findings and policy prescriptions on the most important foreign policy topics; and providing up-to-date information and analysis about world events and American foreign policy on its website, CFR.org.

The Council on Foreign Relations takes no institutional positions on policy issues and has no affiliation with the U.S. government. All views expressed in its publications and on its website are the sole responsibility of the author or authors.

The Council on Foreign Relations sponsors Independent Task Forces to assess issues of current and critical importance to U.S. foreign policy and provide policymakers with concrete judgments and recommendations. Diverse in backgrounds and perspectives, Task Force members aim to reach a meaningful consensus on policy through private deliberations. Once launched, Task Forces are independent of CFR and solely responsible for the content of their reports. Task Force members are asked to join a consensus signifying that they endorse "the general policy thrust and judgments reached by the group, though not necessarily every finding and recommendation." Each Task Force member also has the option of putting forward an additional or a dissenting view. Members' affiliations are listed for identification purposes only and do not imply institutional endorsement. Task Force observers participate in discussions, but are not asked to join the consensus.

For further information about CFR or this Task Force, please write to the Council on Foreign Relations, 58 East 68th Street, New York, NY 10065, or call the Communications office at 212.434.9888. Visit our website, CFR.org.

This report is printed on paper that is FSC® Chain-of-Custody Certified by a printer who is certified by BM TRADA North America Inc.

TASK FORCE MEMBERS

Task Force members are asked to join a consensus signifying that they endorse "the general policy thrust and judgments reached by the group, though not necessarily every finding and recommendation." They participate in the Task Force in their individual, not their institutional, capacities.

Chike Aguh★
EveryoneOn

Edward Alden
Council on Foreign Relations

Eric R. Biel★
Fair Labor Association

Allen Blue
LinkedIn

John Engler
Michigan State University

Diana Farrell
JPMorgan Chase Institute

Kian Gohar★
XPRIZE Foundation

Gordon Hanson
University of California, San Diego's School of Global Policy and Strategy

Robert M. Kimmitt
WilmerHale

Susan Lund
McKinsey Global Institute

Jack Markell

Jamie P. Merisotis
Lumina Foundation

Rodrick T. Miller★
Ascendant Global

Eduardo J. Padrón
Miami Dade College

Penny Pritzker
PSP Partners

Cecilia E. Rouse★
Princeton University's Woodrow Wilson School of Public and International Affairs

Lee J. Styslinger III
Altec Inc.

Hemant Taneja
General Catalyst Partners

Laura Taylor-Kale
Council on Foreign Relations

★The individual has endorsed the report and signed an additional or dissenting view.

iii

CONTENTS

FOREWORD

The nature of work is undergoing a fundamental shift, one largely brought about by new technologies including but not limited to artificial intelligence, robotics, and autonomous vehicles. In the process, jobs will be both eliminated and created.

For the United States, this is something of a mixed blessing. With the world's most innovative economy, the country is well positioned to exploit (in the best sense) the promise of new technologies and their applications. At the same time, it is painfully clear that American society is ill prepared for this technological transformation because educational opportunity and attainment vary widely and work is the basis for much of a citizen's income, benefits, and, in many cases, self-esteem.

The report of this Independent Task Force rightly focuses on the need to rebuild the links among work, opportunity, and economic security for Americans. It puts forward a number of policy prescriptions for government, business, educators, and nongovernmental institutions.

Americans will need to reimagine their careers; the average worker will know over a dozen separate jobs during his or her lifetime. Citizens will also need to rethink education, jettisoning the notion of education as something largely completed before they enter the workforce. Instead, lifelong learning and periodic retraining will become the new normal. And Americans, together with government at every level, will need to restructure the relationship between jobs and benefits. With much of actual and projected job growth in part-time, contingent, or gig employment, it no longer makes sense to tie employment benefits such as retirement and sick leave to particular jobs. Rather, portable systems of employment benefits should be introduced that follow the individual from job to job.

I want to say something about why the Council on Foreign Relations (CFR) has undertaken this project. This is not the first time a Task Force has tackled a set of concerns outside what is traditionally thought of as national security. In recent years, we have focused on such issues as noncommunicable diseases, K-12 education, and immigration reform and what each of them meant for national security. What is clear is that failure to meet the challenges posed by new technologies will likewise affect U.S. national security, in this case by increasing political pressures for American retrenchment, the consequences of which would be a more unstable and less prosperous world. In addition, the country will have neither the resources nor the political bandwidth to play a large global role if society is in turmoil. In such a situation, populism would be sure to grow, as would opposition to both immigration and trade despite their record of contributing to the country's prosperity.

One important recommendation of the Task Force is to create a National Commission on the U.S. Workforce to carry out research, share best practices, and conduct public outreach on workforce challenges. Notwithstanding this suggestion, the challenges associated with new technologies are in no way limited to Americans. Technology will challenge the unity and stability of countries everywhere, developed and developing alike. There thus needs to be an international component to the response to new technologies. The future of work should become an enduring part of the Group of Twenty agenda, with a mechanism established that enables best practices to be shared.

I would like to thank the Task Force chairs, John Engler and Penny Pritzker, for their significant contribution to this important project. Both were generous and then some with their time and energy. My thanks extend to all the Task Force members for similarly lending their knowledge and experience. The national debate will be considerably strengthened as a result.

This report would not be possible without the supervision of Anya Schmemann, CFR's Independent Task Force Program director, who ably guided this project, as well as CFR's Senior Fellow Edward Alden and International Affairs Fellow Laura Taylor-Kale, who directed the Task Force and coauthored this report. They too have earned our thanks for taking on so complex and critical a subject.

Richard N. Haass
President
Council on Foreign Relations
April 2018

ACKNOWLEDGMENTS

This report is the product of a dedicated effort by a diverse and talented group to understand and offer practical solutions to one of the most important challenges facing the United States. We are grateful for the time, guidance, and expertise the Task Force members and observers provided; it was a pleasure to work with such a knowledgeable and committed group of individuals. In particular, we thank our co-chairs, John Engler and Penny Pritzker, whose leadership and energy motivated this endeavor and pushed the group to develop creative and actionable responses to this ongoing challenge. It has been a privilege to work with them.

The report benefited from input gained through briefings, phone calls, and emails with numerous individuals and organizations. These include but are not limited to: AT&T, Burning Glass Technologies, the Business Roundtable, Google, IBM Corporation, LinkedIn, the Markle Foundation, the National Governors Association Center for Best Practices, Toyota, the United States Conference of Mayors, Walmart, Byron Auguste, James Bessen, Wesley G. Bush, Jacqui Canney, Scott Cheney, Aneesh Chopra, Thomas F. Cooley, J.P. Eggers, John Fischer, Alastair Fitzpayne and Anna Fife, David Goldston, Anat Lechner, Suzan G. and Eric A. LeVine, Andrew McAfee, Patrick McKenna, Tom M. Mitchell, Jon Schnur, Robert Seamans, and Meredith Sumpter. We also thank those who reviewed and commented on the draft, including Molly Elgin-Cossart, James M. Goldgeier, Marie T. Lynch, Bhakti Mirchandani, and Anthony Wayne. Special thanks to Jim Hock for his valuable input and support throughout the process. While we sought the advice and input of many, we take responsibility for any errors or omissions in the final text.

We have many to thank at CFR. Independent Task Force Program

Director Anya Schmemann led our team flawlessly in coordinating the meetings, drafting, editing, and outreach for the report; Program Coordinator Chelie Setzer provided invaluable support in coordinating this project and did careful edits of many drafts. We are grateful to the Publications team for editing and preparing the report for publication and to the Digital team for designing the report and producing the graphics in the text. Research Associate Shelton Fitch provided crucial research, editing, and organizational support, as did interns Jonathan Coutinho, Blake Ledna, Maureen McGinn, and Ellen Myers. We also appreciate the feedback from CFR members who participated in events over the course of this project, and our thanks extend to the CFR teams who facilitated those gatherings.

Finally, we are grateful to CFR President Richard N. Haass for giving us the opportunity to direct this project and for his continued focus on this issue.

Edward Alden
Project Director

Laura Taylor-Kale
Deputy Project Director

INDEPENDENT
TASK FORCE REPORT

EXECUTIVE SUMMARY

The world is in the midst of a profound transformation in the nature of work, as smart machines and other new technologies remake how people do their jobs and pursue their careers. The pace of change will almost certainly accelerate, and the disruptions will grow larger. In the United States, where work is the basis for most of the income and benefits that make a secure life possible for Americans and their families, the transformation has been especially wrenching. Even with the reasonably strong job growth of recent years, the divide between those succeeding and those struggling is growing, regional disparities are increasing, economic inequality is rising, and public anger is deepening political divisions.

The challenge facing the United States today is to rebuild the links among work, opportunity, and economic security for all Americans in the face of accelerating technological change. Governments, businesses, educators, and other institutions need to do far more to help Americans adapt and thrive in the face of these disruptive forces. Failure to do so will increase the pressures for retrenchment that are already causing the United States to back away from global leadership. A United States that cannot provide better job and career options and greater economic security for its citizens will be less competitive and less of an example to the world. It will have fewer resources available for national security. Domestic struggles over the sharing of economic gains will further distract and divide the country, and make it less willing and less able to act effectively in the world.

As technology disrupts industry after industry, the United States needs better ways to help Americans access the many new opportunities technology is also creating, in particular by strengthening the link between education and employment prospects. The country needs stronger support for job creation, especially for better-paying jobs. It needs to make the skill demands of jobs much more transparent, so job seekers know the credentials required to move ahead on their own career paths. It needs to ensure that all Americans can gain the skills and knowledge that they—and the economy—depend on for success. And the United States needs to improve the benefits and returns from work for all Americans.

The United States has a proud history of economic leadership. It was the first country to offer public high school education to all its citizens and the first to open the door widely to postsecondary education. It became the manufacturing powerhouse of the world and led the writing of economic rules that helped spread the benefits of economic growth globally. It has continued to lead in the development of new and even wondrous technologies that have the potential to nurture smarter, healthier, and more enriching lives for people across the world. But to prosper and to lead, the United States needs to find new ways to meet the workforce challenges of the twenty-first century.

The seven major findings of the Task Force are:

- Accelerating technological change will alter or eliminate many human jobs. Although many new jobs will be created, the higher-paying ones will require greater levels of education and training. In the absence of mitigating policies, automation and artificial intelligence (AI) are likely to exacerbate inequality and leave more Americans behind.

- Embracing technological innovation and speeding adoption are critical for U.S. national security and economic competitiveness. Openness to

INTRODUCTION

The most important challenge facing the United States—given the seismic forces of innovation, automation, and globalization that are changing the nature of work—is to create better pathways for all Americans to adapt and thrive. The country's future as a stable, strong nation willing and able to devote the necessary resources and attention to meeting international challenges depends on rebuilding the links among work, opportunity, and economic security.

U.S. success in the twentieth century was built on the foundation that hard work and commitment by its citizens would be rewarded with jobs that provided reasonable material comfort, prospects for advancement, and a secure retirement. That promise—of a life in which work offers opportunity and a measure of financial security—has eroded for too many, undermining faith in American institutions and weakening support for strong U.S. global leadership.

It took nearly a decade after the start of the Great Recession in 2008 for the unemployment rate to fall to its prerecession level, the slowest recovery since the Great Depression. Even with the continuing, steady recovery, the percentage of Americans working has fallen significantly, and many are still working only part-time or are marginally attached to the labor force.[1] Far too many of the jobs created over the past decade have been lower-wage and part-time positions, many without the health care, paid leave, and retirement benefits that have long been the hallmarks of stable and secure employment. The lingering effects of the recession varied hugely across the country as well, with coastal and technology-based cities mostly recovering quickly and much of the industrial Midwest and South lagging.[2] The relationship among work, opportunity, and economic security has been undermined for too many Americans, contributing to a spreading discontent and disillusionment that is damaging the fabric of the country.

The United States today faces an enormous twin challenge: creating new work opportunities, better career paths, and higher incomes for its people, while developing a workforce that will ensure U.S. competitive success in a global economy that will continue to be reshaped by technology and trade. If the United States cannot find ways for its companies to succeed *and* for its workforce to share more fully in that success, the political pressures for retrenchment—including trade protection, immigration restrictions, and possibly even restraints on technology and automation—will grow.[3] The result will be an economically weaker, less confident, more divided, and more vulnerable United States, one that will retreat from global leadership. The consequences of such retrenchment will be a more unstable and less prosperous world—undoing the enormous gains made over the past seventy-five years. A United States that does not offer paths to success for more of its own people will harm not only its own prospects, but those of other countries as well.

The links among work, opportunity, and economic security have been weakening steadily for decades, and more precipitously in the twenty-first century. Real wages for Americans in the middle of the income distribution are up a mere 3 percent since 1979, and those at the bottom have lost ground.[4] Inequality has widened more sharply than in any other advanced economy, with the gains accruing especially to the wealthiest; the difference in earnings between Americans in the top 10 percent of the wage pyramid and those in the bottom 90 percent has more than quadrupled since the late 1970s.[5] The effects are lasting from generation to generation. In 1970, more than 90 percent of thirty-year-olds earned more than their parents had at the same age; today that number is barely half.[6] And the trends have worsened over time; some 80 percent of U.S. households saw their incomes fall or remain flat in the decade after 2005, even as costs of such necessities as education, housing, and health care rose.[7]

Why has the link between work and rewards weakened? There is no single cause, but three in particular stand out—the rapid pace of technological change, heightened global competition, and growing barriers to opportunity.

Technology has long been the great engine of American prosperity, and the United States today remains the most innovative economy in the world.[8] Innovation and the spread of technology are the drivers of productivity growth and the foundation for rising living standards, but advances in computing and robotics have also made it increasingly possible for companies to replace human labor with machines. While many new opportunities will likely be created to replace those lost, American workers face big obstacles in acquiring the education and skills needed to prosper in a more automated work environment. While there are different predictions about the pace and scale of the coming technological disruption that will be brought by artificial intelligence, driverless vehicles, and other breakthroughs, there is widespread agreement that disruption will increase. As many as one-third of American workers may need to change occupations and acquire new skills by 2030 if automation adoption is rapid, according to an estimate by McKinsey Global Institute (MGI).[9]

Trade expansion has similarly brought many benefits to the U.S. economy, creating new markets, attracting foreign investment, and lowering the prices of consumer goods, from clothing to food to the latest generation of smartphones. And it has benefited the world. More people—both in absolute numbers and as a percentage of global population—were lifted up from extreme poverty over the last two decades than in any other period in human history, with the poorer countries closing the income gap with their wealthier counterparts.[10] Most of the gains came in countries that opened themselves to global commerce. But trade has also placed American workers in competition with overseas workers earning much less, and has freed up U.S.

companies to invest and expand on a global basis. That has diminished prospects for some Americans, especially with the disappearance of manufacturing jobs that once provided a path to the middle class for those with modest levels of education.[11] The United States lost some six million manufacturing jobs in the 2000s before recovering slightly in recent years; the remaining twelve million manufacturing jobs today

As many as one-third of American workers may need to change occupations and acquire new skills by 2030 if automation adoption is rapid.

account for less than 10 percent of nonagricultural employment.[12] Intense international competition is likely to continue due to the global nature of supply chains in so many industries.

Growing barriers to opportunity have also increased the obstacles for those seeking work. Occupational licensing has exploded: in 1950 only one in twenty American workers needed an occupational license; today one in four does. And most of these licenses are issued by states and are not automatically recognized by other states.[13] Restrictive zoning has prevented the expansion of housing in many of the large cities where job opportunities are growing fastest. Public subsidies for housing have shrunk, and lack of investment in transportation infrastructure makes it harder for employees to commute long distances so they can live in cheaper housing. High-speed broadband, the arteries of the modern information-services economy, is still unavailable in many parts of the country, cutting people off from many of the opportunities of the twenty-first-century economy. And new business start-ups have slowed, diminishing the number of young, fast-growing companies that were once engines of job growth.

Unfortunately, too many U.S. political and business leaders were late in recognizing and responding effectively to these growing challenges. Many state and local governments are experimenting—often in close cooperation with nonprofit groups and foundations—with creative responses in education, worker retraining, apprenticeships, and local economic development initiatives. But these efforts have not reached critical mass across the country. Some employers are finding ways to tackle their own workforce challenges, often in the absence of supportive government policies, but self-help is usually beyond the reach of smaller companies. Federal policy has failed to keep pace with a changing economy and is doing far too little to help Americans navigate the new challenges. An effective response will require concerted action by all levels of government, as well as action by companies, educational institutions, foundations, labor unions, and others.

Work is important not only for people's economic success but also for its ability to provide purpose and meaning, self-respect and dignity; work builds communities and allows individuals to contribute to the larger well-being of society. Every American should have the opportunity and resources needed to prepare for and pursue work that offers them a fair chance at both economic security and meaningful contributions to society. The United States should dedicate itself urgently to rebuilding the links among work, opportunity, and economic security for Americans.

FINDINGS
Technology and Work

Accelerating technological change, including automation and advances in artificial intelligence that can perform complex cognitive tasks, will alter or replace many human jobs. While many new jobs will be created, the higher-paying ones will require greater levels of education and training. In the absence of mitigating policies, automation and artificial intelligence are likely to exacerbate inequality and leave more Americans behind.

Technology has been the biggest cause of job disruption in recent decades, and the pace of change is likely to accelerate. Computers and robots can now recognize and respond to human speech and translate languages; they can identify complex images such as human faces; they can steer cars and trucks; they can perform medical diagnoses and assist in surgical procedures. The United States has already been living through the era of machines replacing physical labor; a typical U.S. steel mill today produces five times as much steel per employee as it did in the early 1980s, and productivity gains are similar across other leading goods-producing industries. Computers have also replaced or altered many routine service occupations, including travel agent, switchboard operator, secretary, and file clerk. In the coming era, computers will augment or replace tasks in many cognitively based occupations as well, from legal research to medical diagnosis to financial advice, and machines with the capacity to learn will get better at these tasks over time. Advances in artificial intelligence will mean that machines will become able to outperform humans in areas of perception (as seen with driverless cars) as well as pattern recognition and calculation (which will aid medical diagnosing). Digitalization of the workplace has already been transformational—as Mark Muro and his colleagues at the Brookings Institution have put it, computerization is "like steam power or electricity, so broadly useful that it reorients the entire economy and tenor of life." They estimate that in the twenty-first century the number of U.S. jobs requiring high levels of digital skills has more than quadrupled already, from 5 to 23 percent of total employment—about thirty-two million jobs—while the number of jobs requiring little in the way of digital skills has fallen from 56 percent to less than 30 percent.[14]

Is the United States facing a coming age of mass unemployment, in which machines will do most of the work once reserved for human beings? The most dramatic estimates have suggested that nearly half of all jobs in the United States could be replaced by automation, and the effects would be felt more acutely by those with lower levels of education.[15] Research by MGI suggests a narrower but still significant result; about 5 percent of occupations could be fully automated with existing technologies, but most occupations will still be affected in some way by automation. The MGI study estimates that in about 60 percent of all occupations, especially more routine jobs, at least 30 percent of job tasks are potentially automatable.[16] Occupations that are especially

Nearly two-thirds of the 13 million new jobs created in the U.S. since 2010 required medium or advanced levels of digital skills.

vulnerable include manufacturing, food service, and retail trade; the White House Council of Economic Advisers has estimated that more than 80 percent of jobs paying less than twenty dollars per hour could be automated.[17] Nearly three million Americans drive trucks for a living, for example, and could lose their jobs as self-driving vehicles are more widely deployed. Nearly five hundred thousand brick-and-mortar retail jobs have been lost over the past fifteen years, while the expansion of e-commerce has created fewer than two hundred thousand new jobs.[18] Nearly 25 percent of African American workers are concentrated in

Figure 1. PROJECTED GROWTH FOR
THE TOP TEN U.S. HYBRID JOBS

Hybrid jobs require proficiency in both business and technology skill sets, for which education and training have traditionally been separate.

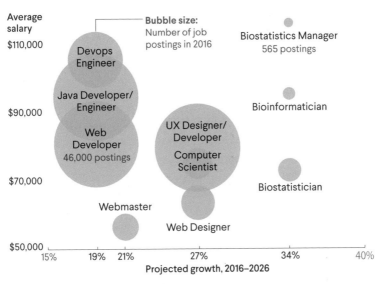

Source: Burning Glass Technologies, 2016.

a handful of occupations that are highly susceptible to automation, such as retail salesperson, cook, and security guard.[19] But automation will also affect better-paid occupations, such as financial analyst, doctor, lawyer, and journalist. Any work tasks that can be routinized even in part are subject to replacement by computers or robots, and advances in artificial intelligence will steadily increase the number of occupations affected.[20]

Whether these technologies will destroy more jobs than they create is impossible to know with any certainty. Data are currently inadequate on how workplaces are adopting and incorporating emerging technologies. Economic history suggests that technological advancements spin off new forms of work; the occupation of web developer, for example, did not exist until the early 1990s, and last year employed 150,000 Americans at a median salary of $66,000.[21] Self-driving cars and smart technologies will require human maintenance and repair, creating new blue tech jobs for those with sophisticated repair skills. In the two decades ending in 2012, employment actually grew faster in fields that were being rapidly computerized, such as graphic design, than in those that were automating more slowly.[22] The new technologies are also coming into the workplace at a time when the workforce is aging rapidly and new positions are opening due to retirements; the graying of the baby boom generation has even led some employers to try to retain their older workforce past normal retirement age.[23]

There is far more agreement that technology already has caused, and will continue to contribute to, polarization of the workplace. Occupational structure has been polarizing in all the advanced economies.[24] Nearly two-thirds of the thirteen million new jobs created in the United States since 2010, for example, required medium or advanced levels of digital skills; mean annual wages in the highly digital occupations are more than double those in occupations that require only basic digital skills. Basic familiarity with spreadsheets, word processing, and customer relationship management software is becoming a baseline requirement for many positions.[25] A distressing shortage of women and minorities acquire these middle and advanced digital skills, leading to still more wage disparity. In addition to the demographics of aging, employers need to take full advantage of the diversity of the U.S. population to maximize their success and to solve problems with the nation's full creative capacity.

As technological sophistication increases the complexity of work environments, demand is growing for employees who excel at skills that machines cannot replicate, at least currently: empathy, teamwork, collaboration, problem solving, critical thinking, and the ability to draw connections across disciplines. Many of the higher-paying new jobs are based on creativity and successful interaction with colleagues rather than on more efficient accomplishment of a narrow set of tasks. As the cognitive capabilities of machines expand, technical education in science, technology, engineering, and math (STEM) will increasingly need to be supplemented with design thinking, entrepreneurship, and creativity, areas where Americans excel.[26] More Americans will need to complete postsecondary education. Occupations that require a college education or advanced degree will grow over the next decade and beyond, whereas employment in occupations requiring only a high school education or below will decline.[27]

Concerns over technology-led disruption are far from new.[28] Economist John Maynard Keynes warned in 1931 of widespread unemployment owing to technology.[29] In 1966, the National Commission on Technology, Automation, and Economic Progress, established by Congress during the Lyndon B. Johnson administration, said that "the fear has even been expressed by some that technological change would in the near future not only cause increasing unemployment, but that eventually it would eliminate all but a few jobs, with the major portion of what we now call work being performed automatically by machine."[30] The evidence does not suggest the United States is today, any more than it was in 1931 or 1966, on the cusp of an era of widespread, technology-induced unemployment. A more moderate view predicts that some jobs will be lost due to automation, and the adjustment will be especially challenging because many of the new jobs being created will require significantly higher levels of education and skills. In the absence of countervailing efforts, more Americans are likely to be pushed into lower-wage work.

Whether adoption proceeds rapidly or moderately, many workers will need to adapt to changing work tasks or switch to new occupations entirely. A policy of waiting and hoping that the market will sort out the challenges, however, is not an adequate response. Failure to provide the education, training, and resources that Americans need to seize these new opportunities, and to use policy tools to spread the benefits of technology more widely, will leave millions of Americans to face lives of diminishing prospects.

Innovation
and Competitiveness

Embracing technological innovation and speeding adoption
are critical for U.S. national security and economic competitiveness. Openness to trade and immigration are also vital
for maintaining U.S. technological leadership.

While technological change presents significant economic and social
challenges, preserving technological leadership remains vital to U.S.
national security and economic competitiveness. If the United States
loses its technological edge, its standing in the world will be threat-
ened. U.S. rivals understand this clearly; China's push for "indige-
nous innovation" and its Made in China 2025 plan for $300 billion in
government-directed subsidies are aimed at making China a world
leader in advanced technologies such as artificial intelligence, electric
cars, 5G mobile communications, and bioengineering.[31] In July 2016,
Beijing outlined an ambitious plan to become the world's leader in
artificial intelligence by 2030, surpassing the United States. China has
also advanced mobile internet and applications at a staggering pace and
now seeks to export them to the world. If successful, these initiatives
would both bring huge commercial gains to China and also help build
the capability for China to rival the United States militarily.

The good news is that the United States is still the world's leader in
the development and diffusion of new technologies. Total U.S. R&D
funding reached an all-time high of nearly $500 billion in 2015, nearly
3 percent of U.S. gross domestic product (GDP), with 60 percent of

that coming from the private sector.[32] The United States has all the right ingredients to remain a technological leader—an entrepreneurial culture, a favorable regulatory environment, a developed venture capital industry, and most of the world's leading research universities.[33] It can and should continue to build on those strengths.

There are some worrisome signs, however. Federal funding for R&D, which goes overwhelmingly to basic scientific research, has declined steadily and is now at the lowest level since the early 1950s, even as other countries, such as Brazil, China, Singapore, and South Korea, are accelerating their investments.[34] State government support for public research universities has also fallen sharply because of state budget constraints.[35] Some nations are inducing or pressuring U.S. companies to transfer technologies and manufacture these innovations locally as the price of investing.[36] A 2013 commission led by Jon Huntsman, the current U.S. ambassador to Russia, and Admiral Dennis Blair, the former director of national intelligence, found that intellectual property theft was costing the United States hundreds of billions of dollars each year and seriously eroding its innovative edge.[37]

Public concerns about technology are also growing. An October 2017 Pew Research Center poll found that three-quarters of Americans are worried about a future in which computers and robots will do many jobs, fearing that job prospects will diminish and economic inequality will worsen.[38] Fortunately, there are so far few signs of any concerted efforts to retard the adoption of technology. Microsoft cofounder Bill Gates's proposal for a tax on robots that replace human workers found few backers; the European Parliament in 2017 rejected a similar proposal to tax robots to pay for retraining workers they displace.[39] If regulations were adopted to discourage new technologies, they would harm U.S. economic prospects. Those companies that have been the most aggressive in disseminating new digital technologies, for example, have grown faster than companies that have been slower to digitize. MGI estimates that the United States has captured only 18 percent of its potential from digital technologies in terms of faster growth, higher productivity, and benefits to consumers.[40] The United States has benefited immensely from the success of its high-technology clusters in the Research Triangle Park in North Carolina, Route 128 in Boston, Silicon Valley, and dozens of other innovation hub cities across the country, such as Ann Arbor, Austin, New York, and San Diego. These are successes that the rest of the world is still trying to emulate. But without policies that continue to promote the development and rapid commercial adoption of technological advances, the United States risks falling behind in the competitive global landscape.

Accessing the fast-growing overseas markets and welcoming talented immigrants from around the world are also vital to U.S. success in the economic race of the twenty-first century. The most successful American companies are operating on a global scale, investing and selling their goods and services both overseas and in the United States. Washington needs to do more to enforce strong trade rules, intellectual property protection, and labor standards in trade agreements and trade preference programs. The trade agenda should also include a concerted effort to press other countries to raise wages in order to create new sources of growth for the world economy. But a United States that turns its back on trade opening—as the Donald J. Trump administration did by walking away from the Trans-Pacific Partnership (TPP) agreement in the Asia-Pacific and threatening to leave the North American Free Trade Agreement (NAFTA) with Canada and Mexico—will seriously diminish prospects for its best companies and for its workforce.

Immigration restrictions, particularly on highly skilled migrants, would be similarly harmful. American universities still attract the lion's share of the best foreign students, and immigrants have played vital roles as entrepreneurs and engineers in Silicon Valley and other U.S. innovation hubs.[41] But there are worrisome signs of a drop-off in foreign student enrollment, and the Trump administration has been rolling out a series of measures that will make it increasingly difficult for highly skilled immigrants to work in the United States.[42] At the same time, China is opening its doors wider than ever before to foreign workers, especially those with science and technology training.[43] The United States today is in a global competition to attract and

Figure 2. RESEARCH AND DEVELOPMENT EXPENDITURES BY U.S. BUSINESS AND THE FEDERAL GOVERNMENT

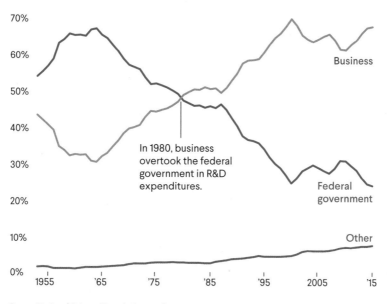

In 1980, business overtook the federal government in R&D expenditures.

Source: National Science Foundation, 2018.

retain the best immigrants and should embrace policies that seek to enhance the economic contributions of immigrants, rather than seeing them as competition for scarce U.S. jobs. If the country fails to win that competition, it will lose investment, jobs, and growth.

U.S. entrepreneurship also needs to be revitalized. The rate of new company formation has been slowing for decades, and that slowdown has accelerated since the turn of the century, likely driven by lack of access to capital and the growing dominance of a smaller number of large companies.[44] Fewer young companies are reaching the stage of rapid and explosive growth that has in the past been such a big contributor to job creation.[45] The slowdown has been especially evident outside high-growth cities; from 2010 to 2014, even as the economy was recovering, counties with one hundred thousand or fewer residents lost more businesses than they created.[46]

Technology does not see borders. In the absence of a workforce with the right skills and opportunities, without a regulatory regime that favors innovation, without access to global markets, and without state and local policies that favor the development of successful clusters, the United States will not realize its full potential in the economy of the twenty-first century. U.S. companies, as well as its smartest scientists and innovators, can move internationally to take advantage of opportunities and better enabling environments, whether the quality of the workforce or the regulatory environment. The best and the brightest can choose other countries to launch and build their businesses. The loss of technological leadership would weaken U.S. national security and diminish economic prospects for Americans. The United States should find new ways to expand its technological leadership while creating better employment opportunities for more Americans.

Growth and Income

Strong economic growth that leads to full employment has been the most consistently successful approach for raising the wages of Americans.

Strong and sustained economic growth is needed to create better job opportunities in the future. Any discussion about the jobs of the future will be moot if the economy is not growing rapidly enough to create many new jobs. Economic policies that maintain strong growth and full employment are therefore needed just to set the table to meet the deeper challenges brought on by rapid technological change. Over recent decades, periods of strong growth have been the few bright spots amid generally discouraging trends in the U.S. labor market.

Wage growth has been weak for U.S. workers for decades now, averaging just 0.2 percent annually since 1973. For wages to grow steadily for most workers, their productivity needs to rise (which comes from better education and training and from investments in new technologies), their share of the gains needs to be stable or rising, and wage gains need to be broadly shared across income groups.[47] Those conditions have not existed in a consistent way for several decades. Improvements in labor productivity, or output per worker, slowed substantially after 1973 and have been particularly anemic for more than a decade. The share of income gains going to the workforce has also fallen. After remaining stable for three decades after World War II, the U.S. labor share of income has fallen as the corporate share has

Figure 3. U.S. WORKERS' SHARE OF NATIONAL INCOME

Full employment in the 1990s pushed up wages, but labor's share of income plummeted in the weak economy of the 2000s.

Source: U.S. Bureau of Labor Statistics, 2017.

grown; labor's income share, which was close to 65 percent in the mid-1970s, is today below 57 percent.[48] U.S. wages used to track quite closely with increases in productivity but began falling behind in the late 1970s. And where labor has made gains, these have overwhelmingly gone to the best-paid workers. Since 1979, wages for those in the top quintile of income have risen 27 percent in real terms, from thirty-eight dollars per hour to forty-eight dollars per hour. But the bottom quintile has seen a slight fall in real wages, and those in the next two brackets have seen little gain.[49] The United States is not alone here: most of the advanced economies have seen rising inequality in wage earnings and a falling labor share of income. But the polarization has been more extreme in the United States than in other similar economies.[50]

The best antidote to these polarizing trends has been a strongly growing economy that is at or near full employment (an economy in which unemployment is low, temporary, and mostly associated with voluntary job changes). Since 1980, the U.S. economy has reached full employment just 30 percent of the time, compared to 70 percent between the late 1940s and 1980, when wage growth was far stronger.[51]

In the aftermath of the Great Recession, it took nearly a decade for the unemployment rate to fall back to the prerecession level. Official unemployment today is near 4 percent, but the broader measure of unemployment, which includes those marginally attached to the labor force and those working part-time who seek full-time employment, is over 8 percent.[52]

Full employment has been the best predictor of wage growth over the past forty years. The strongest period of real wage growth came during the booming economy of the second half of the 1990s. Over the past two years wages have risen faster for lower-wage workers than for higher-wage workers, likely as a result of a tighter labor market and minimum-wage increases in some states and cities.[53] The story is similar in terms of labor's share of the national income. Labor's share fell sharply during the recession of the early 1980s, but then rebounded strongly with the recovery in the second half of the decade. The labor share fell again in the early 1990s, but grew strongly in the last half of that decade to again reach mid-1970s levels; by 2000, unemployment had fallen to just 4 percent and labor force participation hit an all-time record of more than 67 percent. The decline in the labor share of income was steepest in the 2000s, falling throughout the decade and accelerating during the 2001 recession and the Great Recession.[54]

In addition to strong growth, more targeted measures may be needed, particularly to boost earnings for those in service sectors such as health care or retail, where productivity growth has been slower. The U.S. economy has had and will continue to have enormous demand for personal service occupations of all sorts. Jobs for home health and personal care aides, for example, are predicted to grow by 40 percent, or an additional 1.1 million jobs, by 2026. But the median pay is just under $22,000 per year.[55] Other occupations that will see the largest growth in total numbers include generally low-paying jobs such as fast-food worker, cook, janitor, and house cleaner.[56] Compared with those of other advanced economies, the U.S. labor market is particularly polarized—among the Organization for Economic Cooperation and Development (OECD) countries, the United States has a higher share of working poor (defined as earning less than half the median income) than any other country except Greece and Spain.[57] A boost in the minimum wage could benefit some of these workers, as could expansion of the Earned Income Tax Credit (EITC) or other tax policies linked to work. Youth unemployment, which is roughly double the national average, is another area where targeted approaches may be needed. Successful initiatives have included Jobs for America's Graduates, which focuses on reducing high school dropout rates, and Generation, which operates in five countries and ten U.S. cities to offer training in job skills for young people.[58]

Finally, efforts should be made to revitalize struggling communities, many of which boast strong histories of economic success secured through some now-obsolete industry or asset. Often, struggling communities are concentrated in similarly struggling regions—for example, the industrial Midwest and Appalachia—and have high levels of unemployment and disinvestment tied to their former success in now-antiquated industries. Revitalization of these communities hinges on attracting talented and entrepreneurial individuals, facilitating investment in more diverse industries, and ensuring that native residents have access to workforce development and entrepreneurial tools to optimize their productivity. Policies and practices that encourage their homegrown best and brightest to remain are needed if these communities are to be viable over the long term. One in every six Americans is living in an economically distressed community where job prospects have continued to shrink. In these communities—which include large cities such as Buffalo, Cleveland, Detroit, and Newark— employment has continued to fall since the end of the Great Recession. Education is a big divider here; in more prosperous cities, nearly half the residents have a bachelor's degree or higher, whereas in the poorer cities, the figure is just 15 percent.[59]

Immigration could also play a significant role. Canada has pioneered models that allow poorer provinces to attract immigrants who can create new economic activity in their regions. And the sorts of company-educational partnerships discussed below could help make struggling regions a more attractive place for employers to locate. For many companies, the availability of an appropriately skilled and trained labor force is the single greatest factor in determining where to establish or expand operations.

Education, Training, and the Labor Market

> The lack of accessible educational opportunities that are clearly and transparently linked to the changing demands of the job market is a significant obstacle to improving work outcomes for Americans.

The United States became the world's most successful economy in the early twentieth century not just because of its plentiful agricultural land and rich endowment of natural resources, nor simply because of the hard work and entrepreneurial ambitions of its people. The critical ingredient was education. As the huge technological breakthroughs of the era came onstream—including electricity, the automobile, the telephone, and air travel—the demand for a more highly skilled workforce to take full advantage of these new capabilities surged.[60] And the United States responded by far outpacing any other country in expanding high school education to most of its citizens and establishing the state university systems.

From 1910 to 1940, just as modern techniques of mass production were being spread across the country, the number of fourteen- to seventeen-year-old Americans attending high school rose from 18 to 73 percent, and high school completion rose from 9 to 51 percent.[61] No other country even came close to achieving these levels until decades later. Most of the progress was led by state and local governments and citizen groups seized with the urgency of extending free education to as many young people as possible, not by the federal government.

Most of these students did not go on to college but rather went directly into the workforce, with high school completion marking the essential credential needed for most to succeed. After World War II, similar rapid progress was extended to postsecondary education. The GI Bill, passed by Congress in 1944, offered free college education to every one of the nation's sixteen million World War II veterans. The bill, coupled with the spread of affordable, subsidized state universities, allowed both college enrollment and completion to soar.

Today, although the United States has continued to make progress in raising the educational achievements of its citizens, its educators, students, and employers have not adjusted sufficiently to the demands of a changing labor market.[62] Increasingly, the challenge is not just providing more education but providing better-targeted education that leads to better work opportunities, even as the target will continue to shift as new technologies are adopted. The number of job openings nationwide—nearly six million—is near record level, yet many employers say they struggle to find the employees they need.[63] The challenges

The number of job openings nationwide is near record level, yet many employers say they struggle to find the employees they need.

exist not only in higher-paying jobs in information technology and business services, but also in a range of middle-wage jobs, from nursing to manufacturing to traditional trades.[64] The primary focus of the educational system has continued to be formal education for young people—increasing high school completion rates and expanding college enrollment and completion. But that system is too often inadequate in preparing Americans for many of the faster-growing, better-paying jobs in which employers are looking for some mixture of soft skills, specific technical skills, some practical on-the-job experience, and a capacity for lifelong learning. Employers, for their part, have been slow to develop or expand their own training systems to fill in the gaps from the educational system.

While education, appropriately, has many goals beyond just preparing students for the job market, Americans increasingly believe that job preparation is a crucial mission for educators. The 2017 Phi

Delta Kappa poll on attitudes toward public schools found that Americans want schools to "help position students for their working lives after school. That means both direct career preparation and efforts to develop students' interpersonal skills." Specifically, while support for rigorous academic programs remains strong, 82 percent of Americans also want to see job and career classes offered in schools, and 86 percent favor certificate or licensing programs that prepare students for employment.[65]

Making job preparation an education priority will require transformations that are every bit as dramatic as those that came about in the early part of the twentieth century. The goal should be to ensure that all students can develop the knowledge, aptitude, and skills to succeed in a rapidly changing labor market, and are able to continue to build those capacities throughout their working lives. That will require more hands-on involvement by employers and more options outside traditional classroom education—such as apprenticeships—so that students can gain the skills needed for better-paying jobs. Further, addressing this challenge calls for expanded counseling for students to set them on successful education-to-work paths, better credentialing systems to signal market demands more clearly, and transparent data to allow students, employees, and employers to make better educational, career, and hiring choices.

Many Americans have responded to market signals about the value of a college education. Over the past three decades, the earnings gap between those with a college education and those who have only completed high school has doubled.[66] On average, a high school graduate today will earn $1.4 million over the course of his or her life, while the average holder of a bachelor's degree will earn $2.5 million, and the typical professional-degree holder roughly $4 million.[67] Since 1980, the percentage of Americans aged twenty-five and over who have completed four-year college degrees has risen from 17 to 33 percent, a significant increase. Those numbers conceal large inequalities—80 percent of children growing up in the richest 20 percent of U.S. households go to college, and 54 percent complete their degrees on time; for those from the poorest quintile, however, only 29 percent go to college and just 9 percent finish on time.

But the market signal has become less distinct in the twenty-first century. While returns from a four-year degree are still large, real wages for young college graduates—except for those who also have an advanced degree—have risen only slightly since 2000.[68] Disparities in the market value of different majors are huge; the median starting salary for a

Figure 4. *AVERAGE SALARY INCREASE FOR TECHNICAL SKILLS*

The average entry-level salary for a liberal arts graduate is **$42,731.** With the addition of technical skills—such as graphic design, computer programming, or social media—there is a bump in average salary.

Skill set	Salary increase above average
Computer programming	$17,753
Data analysis and management	$12,703
General business	$11,144
Graphic design	$9,188
Social media	$3,424
IT networking and support	$1,058
Marketing	$336

Source: Burning Glass Technologies, 2013.

four-year graduate in computer and information sciences, for example, is more than $71,000, while that for an English major is just over $36,000.[69] Educational institutions will need to get better at tailoring certain programs to labor market signals. Among liberal arts students, for example, those who bolster their education with additional technical skills, such as graphic design, social media, data analysis, or computer programming, roughly double the number of entry-level jobs available to them and can see an estimated $6,000 bump in initial salary.[70] Finally, too many students are borrowing heavily for an education whose returns are unclear. The cumulative debt load for students has more than doubled in the past decade, from $600 billion in 2007 to roughly $1.3 trillion today, while the average debt per student has increased from $15,000 to more than $25,000.[71]

Many excellent career opportunities are also available to those who attend two-year or associate's degree programs; Georgetown University's Center on Education and the Workforce estimates that even with the decline in manufacturing employment, there are some thirty million good jobs in the economy, paying an average of $55,000 per year, for those without a four-year degree.[72] While most colleges have programs leading to work in higher-compensation fields such as technology, engineering, and math, about two-thirds of students at community colleges—and half at for-profit institutions—are enrolled in general studies programs, many in hopes of eventually getting a four-year degree. The majority of community college students say they hope to transfer and complete four-year degrees, but an astonishingly low 12 percent ultimately receive a bachelor's degree.[73] And they are forgoing the opportunity to earn associate's degrees or certificates in well-paid fields such as medical and information technology and business and retail management, where employers say they have a hard time finding qualified candidates.

Other types of education, such as micro-degrees in technology-related occupations, can have real value in the job market with much less upfront investment by students, though they need to be more widely recognized by employers. Online providers such as Coursera and Udacity are expanding their offerings of these sorts of targeted credentials. And work-based learning programs of various types—from traditional apprenticeships to paid internships—can both lower the cost of additional education and help employers develop a pipeline of future employees.

For most Americans, their educational choices will be the most economically consequential decision they make in their lives. They need to be empowered with the resources, information, and opportunities to make the best decisions possible.

> Educational offerings and the employment opportunities available for graduates are too often mismatched. There is a lack of alignment between learning and work that requires better use of data, better career counseling, and more involvement by employers.

Both educators and employers need to participate more effectively in building the workforce of the future. Personnel hiring decisions may be the most important ones that any employer makes, yet most employers make those decisions entirely on the spot market.[74] No company would leave its acquisition of critical raw materials or components to the last moment, but most hiring decisions are made as jobs come open. Employers find themselves competing for often scarce pools of talent, without developing and deepening those talent pools themselves. According to a Harvard Business School survey, just one-quarter of companies have any type of relationship with local community colleges to help prepare employees with the skills they need.[75] Not surprisingly, given their lack of involvement, many companies complain that too few graduates leave school with skills that employers are demanding. A study by IBM, for example, found few courses being offered nationwide in such strong job-growth areas as cloud computing, data analytics, mobile computing, social media, and cybersecurity.[76]

A successful workforce model for the twenty-first century will require a different mind-set. Employers need to think about not just competing for talent, but also how to develop the pipeline of talent they need to build their workforce. That will require greater collaboration

> For most Americans, their educational choices will be the most economically consequential decision they make in their lives.

not just with educational providers but also with other, even competing, employers. Employers should embrace collaborative approaches to talent development; big gains could be made, for example, by industry sectors working together to ensure a steady flow of properly educated and trained students for their future workforce. Educational institutions need to be open to working more closely with employers, without compromising the other elements of their educational mission.

A variety of approaches has proven successful. Many community colleges have been expanding their efforts to partner with employers and to identify in more systematic ways the labor market outcomes for graduates from particular programs. Miami Dade College, for example, has set up programs in animation and game development, working with companies such as Pixar Animation Studios and Google; a program in data analytics, working with companies including Oracle and Accenture; and a physician assistant program, working with local hospitals. Salaries for graduates of these programs far exceed the norm for community college graduates.

Some larger companies are working closely with community colleges and universities to design certificate programs that lead more directly to employment; these programs often include work-study elements that allow students to do internships or apprenticeships at the companies for which they wish to work. Altec, the Birmingham-based provider of trucks, cranes, and other products and services for the telecommunications and electric utility markets, has established close relationships with the educational providers in all its major factory locations. These include many towns and smaller cities, such as Elizabethtown, Kentucky, and China Grove, North Carolina, where finding a skilled labor force within commuting distance can be a challenge. These geographic partnerships, which involve companies, educational providers, and state and local governments, need to be expanded, which will require initiative from the private sector and responsiveness from educational institutions.

Toyota, the Japanese automotive company, has built its own advanced manufacturing technician program to provide a pathway for students seeking careers at the company. The goal is to create a reliable pipeline of "global-quality technical talent" for its U.S. operations, allowing those plants to remain world leaders. The program begins with exposing students in middle and high schools in communities with large Toyota plants, such as Georgetown, Kentucky, to the possibility of a career with the company.[77] Toyota works closely with nongovernmental organizations (NGOs) such as Project Lead the Way to encourage students to acquire the math and science skills they will need. Students who enter the program upon high school graduation undertake a two-year, full-time community college program that mixes school-based learning with paid intern work at the Toyota plant, leading to an associate's degree in applied science that is effectively paid for by the company. Others may go on to complete four-year degrees that can then lead to senior engineering positions in the company. Importantly, the Toyota program is open—other companies seeking employees with similar skills can become involved if they are willing to offer similar work-study opportunities for students. The program is now operating in nine states on twenty-two community college campuses.

Such work-experience programs are too rare—just 20 percent of adults report having received any sort of work experience as part of their education, and most of that was concentrated in health care and teaching.[78] Apprenticeships, which provide work-based education in many technical jobs for those with less than a four-year degree, are relatively rare in the United States; currently there is just one working apprentice for every forty college students in the country.[79] Several million jobs, many of them in career paths leading to higher earnings than traditional apprentice occupations offer, could be opened to apprenticeships.[80] This could also be a cost-saving measure for employers, who often hire four-year college graduates for positions that could be filled by those with a two-year degree plus relevant work experience. Expanding apprenticeships—some of which could serve mid-career workers as well as new trainees—has been a priority for both the Barack Obama and Trump administrations.[81]

Scaling up such efforts is going to require more than just single-company-led initiatives, however. In particular, better data need to be made readily available to colleges and other educational institutions to help them adopt new curricula in a timely fashion, track the labor market outcomes of their students, and then provide that information to prospective students. Students in the Toyota program know with some confidence the value of the degree they will earn. For most students, however, that information is more elusive. While many community colleges try to track the job outcomes of their students, at least in career and technical education (CTE) programs, they rely on surveys with low response rates and rarely track students beyond the first year after graduation.[82] Students need to know with some confidence the market value of particular degrees and certificates, and employers need better ways to signal their demands so potential employees can invest in the skills that are needed. Students need far greater assurance that their investments in education and training—in both time and money—will be rewarded in the job market.

The growth in data about labor market needs and outcomes has been enormous and will only accelerate. The federal government in particular continues to be a critical source of labor market information through its annual randomized surveys, but a growing portion of the data is now in the hands of the private sector, including companies such as Burning Glass Technologies, Indeed, LinkedIn, and Monster. Washington should expand and improve its own data gathering and dissemination, but it also needs to work closely with the private sector to ensure that relevant labor market information is made available quickly to students, educators, and employers.

Significant private-sector and NGO efforts are under way to fill these gaps; the state of Colorado has been a leader here, with a series of education-to-work initiatives supported by the state government, community colleges, employers, data providers, and philanthropic organizations. The U.S. Chamber of Commerce has been pilot testing with several states a jobs registry that is intended to provide much clearer employer information to students, educational institutions, and potential employees about the credentials and competencies that are in demand.[83] The initiative encourages employers to collaborate in forecasting their future workforce needs and create common definitions to signal those needs.

That information, in turn, can help educational institutions develop or expand programs that lead to higher-quality jobs. One big challenge is aligning credentials with employment opportunities. The current market for educational credentials is highly inefficient, with educational providers offering potential students a bewildering array of thousands of degrees, credentials, certificates, and other markers of attainment, often without any clear knowledge about the market value of these credentials. The Lumina Foundation, in cooperation with the Business Roundtable, has funded the Credential Transparency Initiative, with the aim of bringing greater transparency to the credential market. Through an online application called Credential

> Students need far greater assurance that their investments in education and training—in both time and money—will be rewarded in the job market.

Engine, the effort pulls together detailed information about the credential offerings of educational institutions across the country, including cost to acquire, breadth of recognition, and comparisons to offerings at other institutions. Employers, in turn, are able to signal through the registry which credentials they are seeking from future job applicants. Over time, the goal is to produce rich data that allow potential students to assess the labor market value of the credentials offered by different educational institutions.[84] The data will be open-source, allowing for the development of applications to connect credentials with local or sectoral labor market needs.

Similar transparency is needed in the hiring process. Hiring today has moved almost entirely from traditional newspaper ads to online ads, but there is no agreed technical standard for online hiring. Most postings are not presented in a consistent, machine-readable format that allows for easy sharing or developing targeted applications, and many leave out relevant information, such as wages and skills or credentials requirements. Most job ads are available primarily through third-party websites such as Indeed, LinkedIn, and Monster, which makes it difficult to share the announcements broadly or to aggregate the labor market signals they contain.[85] The Obama administration persuaded those companies to cooperate in developing shareable standards for hiring veterans, potentially creating a template for a more open workforce data architecture.[86] Larger efforts are needed. Jobs and hiring information is of such broad value to society—much like weather data—that it should be gathered and shared so the broadest possible use can be made by employers, educational institutions, application developers, and others.[87]

Students also need more active counseling to help them make sensible choices about the relationship between their education and future employment prospects. Small-scale experiments that involve comprehensive advising from college counselors with smaller caseloads and the development of "guided pathways" for students have

A change in thinking is needed, from seeing education and work as distinct and separate activities to considering them as closely linked.

shown dramatic improvements in graduation rates.[88] But the need for good advice goes far beyond the choice of majors or college programs. Almost everyone needs guidance and mentoring to succeed in the labor market; one of the huge advantages that young people from better-off families enjoy is that their parents often have connections to networks of individuals who can open employment doors. Byron Auguste, cofounder of the nonprofit Opportunity@Work, argues that "where the labor market works, it's because people have guidance—from friends, from parents, from mentors. Everyone needs guidance, but some people get it and some don't."[89] As online data about the job market improve, both high school and college counselors will have powerful new tools to help students make better, more cost-effective educational choices. For example, the online portal Journeys—a new application being developed by San Diego-based EDmin—will allow both high school and college students, as well as mid-career workers in transition, to chart various educational paths to achieve their career goals.[90] Such tools will be enormously valuable for both students and guidance counselors to help inform educational choices. More active involvement by employers in educational settings, either directly or through existing structures like state and local workforce boards, and expanded work-based training opportunities would also help transform career advice for students.

Workforce skills are a major competitive issue for the United States. Many of the most productive industries in advanced manufacturing, internet services, and other technology-intensive sectors are highly mobile and capable of being located in many different places in the world. Access to a well-educated, high-quality workforce is critical to these companies. And many countries are simply doing better than the United States in training their workers for these jobs. In Canada and South Korea, for example, more than 60 percent of young people are already graduating from postsecondary programs. The United States, which was the leader in educating its people for much of the twentieth century, now has a lot of catching up to do.

A change in thinking is needed, from seeing education and work as distinct and separate activities to considering them as closely linked. For younger students, that means finding new ways—through work-study programs, early job-oriented counseling, internships, or career-related coursework—to allow them to link what they are learning in school to opportunities in the labor market. For older workers, it means building support for lifelong education to allow them to keep up with the changes that technology will bring.

> Continuing education, retraining, and improvements in skills throughout an individual's working life will be critical to success in the workforce as the rate of technological change increases.

The U.S. educational model—and indeed that of most countries—has long been premised on the idea that young people would acquire a certain level of education in their early years, which would provide the necessary knowledge and credentials to serve them throughout their working lives. In the face of rapid technological change, that notion is increasingly obsolete. Most mid-career employees have already seen their working lives transformed by the introduction of computers and information technology; many administrative jobs, including mail sorter and file clerk, have shrunk rapidly. The promised developments in artificial intelligence are likely to intensify the pace of change, requiring Americans to acquire the knowledge to work with and alongside thinking machines. These pressures are forcing many more American workers to retrain and find new skills more often in their careers, either to advance in their own occupations or to find entirely new ones.

Such transitions are not easy. Like learning a foreign language, embracing new technologies is easier for students and younger workers than it is for older workers. Creating a culture of lifelong learning in the workplace is going to require changes in behavior by companies and their employees, and in many cases will require close cooperation with educational institutions and online education providers. Most institutional and governmental financial support for higher education is aimed at young people; far fewer financing options are available for those looking to upgrade skills, especially if they do not work for a large employer willing to finance some or all of their training. Federal Pell Grants, for example, which are the largest source of federal aid for lower-income students, are not available for those pursuing short-term career-oriented certificates through community colleges and other educational providers.

Some large companies have been pioneering new approaches. AT&T employs some 280,000 people, and their jobs have been transformed over the past two decades as the company has acquired and built out massive wireless networks. That has required employees to develop new skills in cloud-based computing, coding, and other technical capabilities; as one company executive put it, most of the company's employees "signed up for a deal that is entirely different from the environment in which their business operates today."[91] Over the past four years, the company has spent $250 million on employee education, and 140,000 employees have signed up to retrain for the new roles, which they are expected to do on their own time. AT&T has experimented with new forms of education to help employees fit the training into their schedules—it has, for example, teamed up with Georgia Institute of Technology and Udacity to offer an online master's degree in computer science, and Udacity has developed smaller micro-degrees for specialties including coding and web development. Other companies have launched similar initiatives. United Technologies, the parent company of engine maker Pratt and Whitney, has for two decades offered tuition reimbursement of up to $12,000 for employees to pursue part-time degrees.[92]

Retailers, many of which are facing problems with job retention, have launched their own initiatives to challenge the negative perception of retail jobs as dead-end jobs with little possibility for advancement or lateral moves. Costco helps employees who want to rise to management positions return to school to acquire the credentials to move up in the company.[93] Walmart, the nation's largest private employer, with a

> # 60 percent of retail workers are not proficient in reading and 70 percent have difficulty working with numbers.

U.S. workforce of more than 1.3 million, has launched a new wage and training initiative at a cost of nearly $3 billion. Since early 2016, nearly four hundred thousand junior employees have gone through a program called Pathways, which focuses on basic business and math skills, as well as soft skills such as interviewing and interacting with customers. Employees who complete the short program receive a one-dollar-per-hour raise. Additionally, more than 250,000 mid-level managers have graduated from Walmart Academies, which teach advanced retail skills, leadership skills, and specifics of how to run individual store departments.[94] Amazon's Career Choice Program pays up to 95 percent of tuition costs, to a maximum of $2,000, for warehouse employees who have been with the company at least three years and want to learn unrelated skills such as computer-aided design or medical lab technologies.[95] A study by the National Skills Coalition found that 60 percent of retail workers are not proficient in reading and 70 percent have difficulty working with numbers.[96] Several studies have looked at the potential career gains that entry-level retail employees can make from such education and training initiatives at the workplace, and at the value to companies in greater employee retention and improved customer experience.[97] To achieve their real promise, such training initiatives will need to be increasingly collaborative across sectors and employers. The skills developed in retail, for example, could allow employees to make lateral moves into sectors requiring similar skills, such as hospitality and food service.

While such initiatives can and should be embraced by more companies, it is harder for smaller firms to support this sort of retraining. It should be easier for smaller companies to interact with local workforce development boards, community colleges, and even universities to discuss their workforce needs and ways the institutions might be able to help.

Some governments have gone further in trying to expand lifelong-learning opportunities to more of their citizens. Singapore, which has the advantage of being a small country with a population of less than six million, launched its SkillsFuture initiative in 2015, which offers an educational credit for all Singaporeans to return to school if they wish. Singapore also does in-depth analyses of the skills needs of its workforce and tries to target training to meet those needs. The government argues that "with the fast pace of technological advance-ments and stronger global competition for jobs, skills upgrading and deepening are essential for Singaporeans to maintain a competitive edge."[98] If a U.S. state followed Singapore's model, it would likely become a leader in attracting new investment and retaining jobs.

Transition Assistance

U.S. efforts to help workers make the transition from one job or career to another are inadequate. Unemployment insurance is too rigid and covers a fraction of the eligible workforce, and retraining programs such as Trade Adjustment Assistance are not based on the best global models.

In an ideal, full-employment labor market, most job changes would be voluntary, and the period of unemployment would be brief. But policymakers have long understood that the cyclical nature of modern economies often makes full employment an elusive goal. At any given time, millions of people are likely to be out of jobs involuntarily and looking for work, and in times of recession and economic slowdown, those numbers will spike.

In the United States, most of those workers are on their own. The U.S. unemployment insurance (UI) system, which provides temporary income support for individuals after they lose their jobs, was only ever intended to offer some short-term income support while employees moved from one job to the next. The generosity of benefits varies widely from state to state but is generally modest.[99] Many are excluded because they cannot prove they were laid off without cause, or they have simply been out of a job for too long and their benefits have expired. Those employed as independent contractors or working in the gig economy of on-demand work are similarly excluded from UI benefits. The percentage of unemployed workers who are able to collect UI benefits

Figure 5. PUBLIC EXPENDITURES ON ASSISTANCE AND RETRAINING FOR UNEMPLOYED WORKERS IN TOP DEVELOPED ECONOMIES

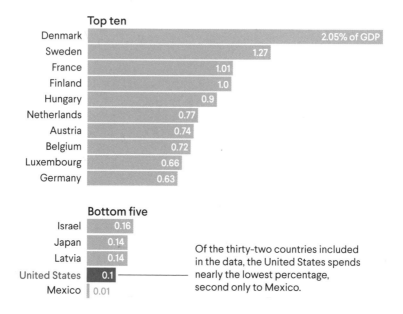

Top ten

Denmark	2.05% of GDP
Sweden	1.27
France	1.01
Finland	1.0
Hungary	0.9
Netherlands	0.77
Austria	0.74
Belgium	0.72
Luxembourg	0.66
Germany	0.63

Bottom five

Israel	0.16
Japan	0.14
Latvia	0.14
United States	0.1
Mexico	0.01

Of the thirty-two countries included in the data, the United States spends nearly the lowest percentage, second only to Mexico.

Source: Organization for Economic Cooperation and Development, 2015.

has fallen from half of all workers in the 1950s to just over one-quarter today.[100] Unemployment insurance no longer serves even the modest function of cushioning income losses for those who are temporarily without work through no fault of their own.

U.S. programs to assist with job transitions have long been recognized as inadequate. In part because the United States generally had much higher levels of labor force participation than most countries in Europe, U.S. policy has put the onus on workers to find new employment with little outside assistance.[101] But U.S. labor participation rates plummeted during the Great Recession and have not fully recovered. According to the OECD, the U.S. employment rate of 72.6 percent is now roughly at the European Union average, and considerably lower than that of the United Kingdom and Germany (77.6 percent) and Canada (78 percent).[102] U.S. government support for retraining for the unemployed is a fraction of that in most other advanced economies: the United States spends roughly one-fifth of what the average European country spends on active labor market programs, which are designed to provide individuals who lose their jobs with the training, skills, and job counseling they need to return to the job market.[103]

The standard program for unemployed workers, the Workforce Investment Act (WIA) of 1998 (updated and renamed by Congress in 2014 as the Workforce Innovation and Opportunity Act [WIOA]), provides minimal assistance for displaced workers. Most are eligible for basic skills assessments and job search assistance, and some get more in-depth job counseling and individualized assistance. Under WIA, those services had to be exhausted before workers were eligible for any sort of education or training that might improve their prospects of finding a better job, and only roughly 5 percent qualified.[104] The system under WIOA is less rigid and some unemployed people can enter retraining more quickly, but federal funding for retraining dislocated workers has been flat, and funding for basic adult education has declined and is likely to face further cuts.[105] More generous support for retraining is available under the Trade Adjustment Assistance (TAA) program for the small number of workers—fifty-five thousand recipients in fiscal year 2016—who can show that they lost their jobs to import competition or outsourcing. But even TAA falls short: the retraining programs too often do not align with local labor market needs, and the subsidy for workers who wish to move to find employment is capped at a mere $1,500, far too small to make a difference. And with more job loss now caused by new technology than by trade competition, having a transition program devoted solely to trade-displaced workers, rather than a broader effort to help displaced workers, makes little sense.[106]

Some U.S. policies have effectively discouraged retraining and reemployment. In communities that were hit hardest by import competition from China in the 2000s, for example, there was a huge increase in the number of workers applying for and receiving Social Security Disability Insurance (SSDI). The costs to taxpayers for SSDI were thirty times as large as expenditures for TAA. And unlike TAA, which is a temporary program, SSDI payments are usually permanent.[107] Under SSDI, workers who show they are unable to return to work for some medical reason are eligible to collect Social Security payments, often for the remainder of their lives. SSDI raises the likelihood of abuse of legally prescribed drugs, because those with ailments may be prescribed opioid-based painkillers whose costs are covered under Medicaid.[108] Drug use then becomes a further hurdle to returning to the job market. Some 4 percent of working-age Americans have already left the workforce through SSDI and related programs.

There are many successful models from elsewhere in the world that have shown success in retraining and quickly moving workers back into the job market. Sweden, for example, has set up Job Security Councils (JSCs) across the country. These are nonprofit organizations run by a board of representatives split equally between employers and employees, financed by a small contribution from employers. The goal of the JSCs is to encourage as seamless a transition as possible for laid-off workers. Employers are required to give significant advance notice of layoffs, and the JSCs then work to provide counseling and guidance—and, if necessary, retraining or business start-up support—to those who are facing job loss. Over 85 percent of Swedish workers are reemployed within a year, the highest percentage in any OECD country.[109] Denmark has a similarly successful system that combines a flexible labor market with relatively low levels of job security (similar to the United States) and generous access to training and reemployment services to help workers get back on their feet.[110]

The U.S. economy would see collateral benefits from stronger transition assistance. In its 2017 employment report, which looks at responses from all the advanced economies, the OECD argues that increased spending on active labor market programs—including job search assistance, wage subsidies, and training—is especially effective at reducing unemployment during economic downturns like the one the United States experienced following the 2008 financial crisis.[111]

Barriers to Employment

Too many jobs are going unfilled because of restrictions related to credentialing, mobility, and hiring practices. More could also be done to help businesses expand and to create new opportunities in higher-unemployment regions.

There are nearly six million job openings in the United States, close to the largest number since the Department of Labor began tracking in 2000. Seven million workers are officially unemployed, and millions of others either are underemployed or have dropped out of the labor market entirely.[112] Many of the challenges of today's workforce concern education, training, and skills, as discussed above. In other cases, employers say they are having difficulty finding employees who can pass drug tests and demonstrate reliable work habits; earlier exposure to the requirements of the workplace in the form of internships that require young people to show up on time and maintain a professional demeanor could help in this regard. But there are also significant "matching" problems—employees who could do the jobs that are open are not in the right places, have earned credentials that are not recognized, or are not being hired even though they have the right capabilities for the job. Broadly speaking, there are three types of matching issues: mobility, occupational licensing, and the hiring process.

Americans used to be among the most mobile people in the world. In 1948, when the Census Bureau began tracking how many Americans move from one place to another each year, it found that more than

20 percent of the country had relocated in the previous year. Those numbers began to fall in the 1980s and 1990s, and then dropped steeply after 2000. Americans relocate in search of new work and career opportunities much less than they once did.[113] That declining mobility appears to be a significant part of why the gap between the richer and poorer states stopped closing in about 1980. For a century prior to that, Americans would move from poorer regions to the wealthier states and cities where jobs were being created, which had the effect of both dampening wage growth in the richer regions and boosting it in the poorer ones.[114]

Declining mobility is a big problem because job growth has become increasingly concentrated. The fastest growth in the country has taken place in the big cities, often those with strong technology economies, such as Boston, Denver, New York, San Francisco, and Seattle, and in energy-strong regions including the Dakotas and Texas.[115] Cities that already have a high concentration of highly skilled jobs are also attracting most of the new highly skilled jobs.[116] The gap between larger cities and smaller ones has been growing, with many smaller cities struggling to recover from the decline in manufacturing employment.[117]

The reasons for the steep decline in mobility are not entirely clear, but there are several likely culprits. Housing prices are clearly a barrier in the largest cities and are exacerbated by land-use restrictions primarily under the control of regional and municipal governments, which impose far more restrictions on housing construction than they once did.[118] While the motivations behind zoning restrictions—to create more livable neighborhoods—are laudable, in the absence of other mitigating policies they have helped drive housing prices into the stratosphere in cities that have seen strong job growth, including Denver, Portland, San Francisco, and Seattle. An absence of affordable housing prevents workers from relocating from lower-productivity regions to higher-productivity regions, which creates significant losses to the U.S. economy.[119] Federal government subsidies for low-income housing have also been shrinking.[120] Transportation infrastructure is another problem. Many job opportunities could be opened up if commuting times were reduced from the outer rings of the large cities, where housing costs are lower; since 2000, a growing number of Americans have found themselves living in towns or suburbs that are beyond the commuting reach of most jobs. The decline in proximity to jobs has been particularly steep for Latinos and African Americans.[121] Overcoming this barrier will require greater investments in all forms of transit, especially mass transit.

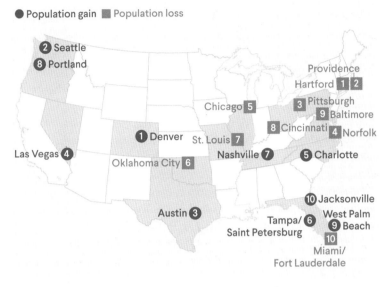

Figure 6. LINKEDIN MEMBERS' MOVEMENT
FOR WORK: CITIES WITH TOP POPULATION GAINS
OR LOSSES IN 2017

● Population gain ■ Population loss

② Seattle
⑧ Portland

Providence
Hartford **1** **2**
3 Pittsburgh
Chicago **5**   **9** Baltimore
8 Cincinnati **4** Norfolk
① Denver   St. Louis **7**
Las Vegas ④
Oklahoma City **6**   Nashville ⑦   ⑤ Charlotte

10 Jacksonville
Austin ③   West Palm
Tampa/ **6**   **9** Beach
Saint Petersburg   **10**
Miami/
Fort Lauderdale

Source: LinkedIn, 2017.

Occupational licensing—most of which is, again, under the authority of state and local governments—is also a significant obstacle that prevents Americans from moving for better work opportunities. The country's three million teachers, for example, need state-issued licenses in order to work in public schools, and in many private schools as well. States often have quite different requirements for obtaining and maintaining teaching credentials, and reciprocity is limited; most teachers who move from one state to another have to meet some additional educational requirement to obtain a certificate.[122] One study of the Pacific Northwest suggested that licensing restrictions meant that teachers near the Oregon border in Washington State were three times as likely to move to another teaching job somewhere else in Washington rather than make the much shorter move across the border to teach in Oregon.[123] Many other occupations—including bartender, interior decorator, cosmetologist, manicurist, and florist—typically require some sort of state licensing that is not generally recognized in other states. Roughly 25 percent of workers today require some sort of state license, compared with just 5 percent in the 1950s.[124] While such credentialing is often necessary to protect consumer health and safety or ensure the high qualifications of individuals doing the work, too often the requirements serve as unreasonable barriers to entry, and the lack of cross-state cooperation in recognizing these credentials is a major obstacle to mobility.[125]

Finally, the hiring process does not function as well as it needs to. Too many college-educated young people are being hired for jobs that do not require four-year degrees; a 2014 Federal Reserve study found that more than 40 percent of recent college graduates were hired for jobs that have not traditionally required a college degree, a figure that has been rising since 2001.[126] Applicant tracking systems, which are widely used by employers to handle the enormous volume of online job applications, are often set up to weed out applicants without college degrees.[127] A Burning Glass study found that 65 percent of current postings for executive secretaries and executive assistants list a bachelor's degree as a requirement, even though just 19 percent of people currently doing those jobs have four-year degrees.[128] Harvard Business School argues that "degree inflation"—in which employers demand four-year degrees for jobs that did not previously require them—"is a substantive and widespread phenomenon that is making the U.S. labor market more inefficient."[129] Americans are excluded from jobs for which they are qualified, and college graduates are underemployed. The effects are particularly negative on populations that have lower-than-average college graduation rates, such as African Americans and Latinos.

Development of industry-wide credentials could help in this regard, as would more active corporate initiatives to develop their own workforce pipelines. But new hiring practices are also needed to help match employees' skills to employers' needs. New digital platforms could do a great deal to solve the matching problem. With platforms such as LinkedIn, job seekers can now search potential openings across the country, and employers have new tools to locate, identify, and screen potential candidates. Such platforms may also facilitate part-time and gig occupations, opening opportunities for those unable or unwilling to pursue traditional full-time employment.[130]

Nongovernmental initiatives such as Skills for Chicagoland's Future and Skills for Rhode Island's Future have demonstrated the benefits of active counseling to match employers with qualified individuals who are unemployed or underemployed.[131] The initiative has been especially focused on the problem of youth unemployment. A 2017 evaluation of the programs showed significant benefits above and beyond the job placement services that WIOA provides.[132] Opportunity@Work is another initiative aimed at expanding tech training and work opportunities to groups that face significant employment barriers, including veterans, people with disabilities, people with limited English proficiency, and those with criminal records.[133] Opportunity@Work, with support from the Department of Labor, is working closely in seventy-two technology communities around the country with employers such as Dell, local workforce development boards, and community colleges to open doors for those who have acquired relevant skills but lack a four-year degree or long work experience that would make them obvious candidates for employers.

Support for Work
in the New Economy

Local, state, and federal governments' existing policies to support work are outdated for the new economy. Current workplace benefits—from sick leave to retirement plans—are too often available only to workers with full-time jobs and are not adapted to the emerging world in which more workers are part-time, contract, or gig workers.

Meeting the growing demand for jobs that require higher levels of education and skills needs to be a priority, but many of the jobs that are and will be created are not traditional, full-time occupations working for a single employer. Workers in alternative arrangements—including independent contractors, freelancers, temporary employees, and gig economy workers—now make up some 16 percent of the total U.S. workforce, a figure that has grown by half over the last decade.[134] Nearly all the net employment growth from 2005 to 2015 came from contingent work.[135] More than 7.5 million workers, most of them low income, hold more than one job. Some of these workers find themselves in precarious "just-in-time" arrangements. Not all of this workforce, by any stretch, is doing such jobs as a last resort. Some may hold part-time positions to supplement their incomes; others, such as young parents, may prefer the flexibility of part-time or gig work. Many Americans no doubt value the flexibility that comes from being able to earn some extra cash by renting out a room through Airbnb or driving for Uber or Lyft. The 2017 tax bill passed by Congress is likely to accelerate the growth of contingent work by providing significant tax savings to independent contractors and freelance workers that are not available to salaried employees.[136]

The growth of both the part-time and contingent workforce, however, points to a huge challenge for the future of the U.S. workforce—the large and growing holes in the support systems for working individuals and families. Since the 1940s, health insurance for American workers has been largely provided by employers and available primarily for full-time employees, as are other benefits including sick leave, family leave, overtime pay, and paid vacations.[137] Retirement benefits are also normally tied to traditional jobs. Contingent and part-time workers are generally not offered company training programs, tuition reimbursement, or loan repayment assistance. Those outside the traditional workforce find themselves in a kind of black hole where they are ineligible for many taxpayer-supported programs that are designed to protect Americans on the job and in retirement, and they have limited prospects for career advancement.

Only two-thirds of private-sector workers, for example, have access to any sort of retirement benefits through their jobs; among the lowest-paid workers, only one-third have such access, and only 14 percent are participating in those plans.[138] Other workplace benefits—including paid sick leave and paid vacation days—are similarly skewed in favor of higher-income workers with full-time jobs. Eighty-four percent of full-time workers are eligible for paid sick leave, for example, but only 36 percent of part-time workers are. Similarly, 92 percent of workers earning in the highest bracket (the top 10 percent) are guaranteed sick leave, but only 31 percent of the lower earners enjoy the same benefit.[139] The United States has especially weak protections for temporary workers compared to other advanced economies, many of which require equal pay rates and the same benefits that are available to full-time employees.[140]

Many of these part-time workers live precarious lives. The most recent study of household economic well-being by the U.S. Federal Reserve found that 30 percent of adults—or seventy-three million Americans—say they are barely getting by financially; among those with a high school degree or less, the figure was 40 percent. Nearly 30 percent of adults say they earn money through "informal" methods to supplement their paid employment. And 44 percent said they would not be able to cover an emergency expense of $400, or would be forced to borrow money or sell something to do so.[141] Many Americans also experience great volatility in their monthly incomes.[142]

The federal and state governments administer a variety of programs that are intended to supplement the incomes of lower-wage workers, including food stamps, Medicaid, and public housing or rent assistance. Many of these programs do help provide an important cushion for low-wage workers. But these are essentially a social-service model, designed to help what is seen as a vulnerable population. The programs should be supplemented by ensuring that the sorts of benefits that better-paid, full-time workers take for granted are similarly available to lower-income, part-time, and contingent workers.

The most urgent need is to expand employment benefits for those who are in nontraditional or part-time work arrangements. The segmentation between full-time work on the one hand and part-time work and independent contracting on the other, in terms of labor market regulations, also encourages some companies to expand the use of contingent workers, in part to avoid the cost of benefits associated with full-time work. If workers were eligible for benefits on a prorated basis, that incentive would be reduced or eliminated. Some states have been considering efforts to implement new systems in which, for example, part-time workers would earn vacation and sick days from one or more employers, which could then be used as needed.[143] New York State has also launched a task force to develop options and recommendations for increasing the portability of benefits.[144] In its recent review of employment policies, the OECD argued that portability should be the model for all advanced economies in the twenty-first century.[145]

The purpose of portable benefits is not just to improve the lives of workers, though that should, of course, be a paramount goal. Initiatives that improve the working conditions for many are also likely to have broader economic payoffs as well. More economically secure workers

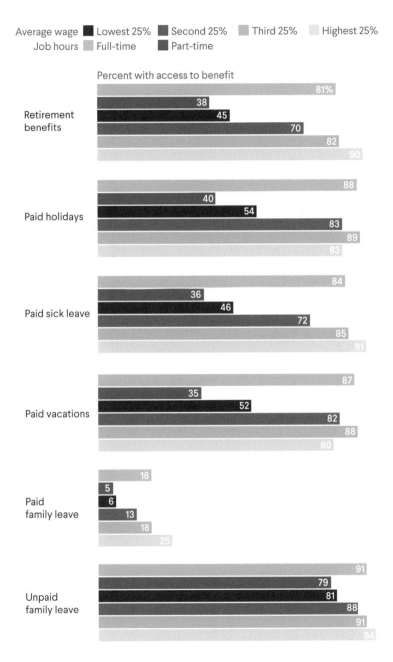

Figure 7. ACCESS TO RETIREMENT AND TIME-OFF BENEFITS IN THE UNITED STATES

Average wage ▮ Lowest 25% ▮ Second 25% ▮ Third 25% ▮ Highest 25%
Job hours ▮ Full-time ▮ Part-time

Percent with access to benefit

Retirement benefits
- 81%
- 38
- 45
- 70
- 82
- 90

Paid holidays
- 88
- 40
- 54
- 83
- 89
- 83

Paid sick leave
- 84
- 36
- 46
- 72
- 85
- 91

Paid vacations
- 87
- 35
- 52
- 82
- 88
- 80

Paid family leave
- 18
- 5
- 6
- 13
- 18
- 25

Unpaid family leave
- 91
- 79
- 81
- 88
- 91
- 94

Source: Bureau of Labor Statistics, March 2017.

are more likely to invest, spend, and boost economic demand, the lack of which has been a primary cause of weak economic growth. Individuals might also feel safer in taking the risk of starting new companies if they were confident they had more secure benefits. The labor legislation of the 1930s, which established a national minimum wage, prohibited child labor, created national unemployment and retirement insurance, implemented the forty-hour workweek, and required overtime pay for many workers, is credited by economic historians with helping to lay stronger foundations for the long prosperity that followed.[146] New initiatives to meet the labor market challenges of the twenty-first century are long overdue.

Next Steps: Building the Foundation for a Stronger United States

Addressing the twin challenges of creating better working opportunities and ensuring competitive success in a global economy reshaped by technology and trade is not just a domestic economic and social challenge for the United States—it is a national security priority. The challenges outlined above influence the United States' ability to act effectively and lead on the world stage. In the face of competing political and economic models, a United States that offers successful paths to opportunity and prosperity for its citizens demonstrates the gains that come from liberal democracy and open markets. In the twenty-first century, the United States should once again lead by example in building the most productive, inclusive, and resilient economy in the world. Building the workforce of the future needs to become an urgent priority, not just in Washington but at all levels of government and across American society.

RECOMMENDATIONS

Creating better work opportunities for Americans, building a well-educated and trained workforce for American employers, and enacting a better set of public policies to support work will require action from governments, businesses large and small, labor unions, nonprofit organizations, and others. It also requires a United States willing to learn from the best examples across the country and around the world. The Task Force recommendations are a launching point for this crucial national effort. They form a suite of options that governments at all levels, employers, educational institutions, and others can enact.

The Task Force recommendations are aimed at rebuilding the links among work, opportunity, and economic security. There need to be clear, understood, and achievable paths by which Americans can pursue better lives for themselves and their families through work. Meeting this challenge requires a commitment at every level of society to invest in and develop the nation's most valuable asset—its people. As President Trump said at the World Economic Forum in January 2018: "To be successful, it is not enough to invest in our economy. We must invest in our people."[147]

The recommendations set out options for local and state governments, the federal government, and other actors, including employers, educational institutions, and nonprofits. Action is critically needed to address each of the challenges detailed above, but the specifics will vary from state to state and institution to institution; different approaches should be encouraged. The Task Force ultimately calls for an overarching national initiative to build and maintain momentum on this vital set of issues.

Three principles should guide the U.S. response to the workforce challenge:

- *Flexibility:* It is difficult to forecast with high confidence how large the scale of workplace disruption will be in the future, or which sectors and occupations will be most affected. Governments, employers, and others should have the flexibility to pursue different approaches and learn from what works best. Initiatives at the state and local level are particularly important to test out new ideas.

- *Transparency:* Although new technologies disrupt traditional work patterns, they also enhance Americans' ability to adapt successfully to change. In particular, big data and other new capabilities, properly harnessed, will allow for better understanding of labor market opportunities, better matching between employees and job opportunities, and better choices on the paths from education to well-paying jobs and careers. New data analysis and more timely and effective data sharing should also allow governments, employers, educators, and individuals to learn more quickly which approaches are the most effective, and to respond accordingly.

- *Resources:* Both governments and companies have failed to invest the resources needed to address these challenges, and they have sometimes targeted resources poorly. The worsening federal budget deficit, which will be exacerbated by the December 2017 tax cuts and the congressional budget agreement, will unfortunately further handcuff the United States in meeting these challenges.[148] Some other advanced economies have responded more successfully to the disruption of work because they have made it a priority and committed resources to address the challenges facing their people. While the particulars of the U.S. response will differ, significant resources are needed to prevent the United States from falling farther behind global competitors. Those resources should be targeted to approaches that have proven successful through experience.

Create Better
Work Opportunities in the
Face of Technological Change

Local and state governments and the federal government should adopt an explicit goal of creating better jobs and career paths for Americans. Initiatives should aim especially at attracting investment and revitalizing entrepreneurship.

Good jobs require a good investment climate. Many large employers today have the ability to locate production facilities anywhere in the world, and the United States is competing with other countries for job-creating investments. Building and maintaining an attractive investment climate should therefore be a priority at all levels of government. The private sector should also undertake initiatives to strengthen the United States as a top global location for business.

Federal government

Reiterate the United States' commitment to maintaining open trade and investment policies. The United States should lay out the welcome mat for foreign investors and underscore its commitment to treating all investors in a fair and equitable manner. Foreign-owned multinational companies have investments worth nearly $3 trillion in the United States, the most of any single country in the world. These firms directly employ more than six million U.S. workers at salaries an average of 25 percent above the U.S. average (about $80,000 per year), and more than one-third of these jobs are in manufacturing. These companies also carry out more than 16 percent of private-sector R&D in the United States.[149] The commitment to openness is vital for U.S.-headquartered multinational corporations as well. U.S.-headquartered multinationals currently employ nearly twenty-seven million Americans at an average annual salary of $77,000. These companies also purchase nearly 90 percent of the inputs from American-based suppliers, creating millions of other good jobs, and account for nearly 90 percent of the private-sector R&D that is critical for maintaining U.S. leadership in innovation.[150] The president should issue a statement committing the United States to maintaining an open investment policy, as every president since Gerald Ford has done.[151]

Maintain a competitive corporate tax rate. The tax reform bill passed by Congress and signed by President Trump reduced the top corporate tax rate from 35 percent to 21 percent, putting the United States in a much better position vis-à-vis its major competitors in the OECD nations. The lower rate—which is now similar to Canada's when federal and state or provincial rates are combined—should help attract more investment to the United States.[152] The United States should, for investment purposes, ensure in the future that its corporate tax rates remain in line with those of its competitors.

Pass a major infrastructure package. This is a stated priority for the Trump administration and should be a priority for Congress. The most urgent needs include expanding broadband coverage and developing "smart cities" and high-speed transportation, as well as maintaining and upgrading existing roads, bridges, and water and sewer systems. The administration has proposed $200 billion in additional federal spending, and hopes to see some $1.5 trillion invested from additional state, local, and private-sector sources, but has also proposed cutting Department of Transportation and other infrastructure funding.[153] Congress will need to find new sources of revenue for infrastructure; it could consider both public-private partnerships and an increase in the gasoline tax, which has not been raised since 1993. The Chamber of Commerce has backed a twenty-five-cent-per-gallon increase in the tax, which would raise about $375 billion over the next decade.[154]

Support U.S. exporters. The Export-Import Bank and other agencies should increase financing for U.S. exporters, with a particular focus on small business. The United States should embrace a renewed, outward-looking trade agenda, and in particular expand export opportunities into fast-growing, developing economies and encourage lower-cost and easier customs processing for access to foreign markets. Digital platforms through companies such as Amazon and eBay can be especially helpful for smaller companies in identifying and serving new overseas customers.

Negotiate with other governments to set parameters for investment competition. While the United States should be aggressive in attracting and promoting investment, there are real dangers of a "race to the bottom" as countries continue to cut corporate tax rates and offer other financial inducements in an effort to attract investment. The United States should cooperate with efforts underway in the OECD, including its base erosion initiative, to establish basic parameters for investment competition.[155] The United States should also move forward with negotiations on stalled bilateral investment treaties, especially with China. This would set clearer terms under which Chinese investment will be welcomed in the United States and when it may be resisted to safeguard national security or prevent an economically harmful transfer of technology. Such a treaty should also be premised on reciprocal access for U.S. companies to pursue investment opportunities in China.[156] As governments around the world consider tightening review mechanisms for foreign investment, the focus should be on identifying true national security concerns so as not to deter job-producing investments.

State and local governments

Adopt best practices in local economic development. All state and local governments should have ambitious local economic development initiatives designed to both attract new investment and build from within. The National Governors Association has spelled out a series of best practices for economic development, including emphasizing job creation from within, supporting local entrepreneurs, strengthening advanced manufacturing, harnessing local universities to help bridge the gap between research and commercialization (often called the "valley of death"), and promoting exports from the region. The goal should be to create hubs that "bring together the critical ingredients for innovation—smart people, research institutions, entrepreneurial training and mentors, and professional networking."[157] These best practice recommendations include the following:

- Regional economic development organizations should develop regional economic strategies that align objectives at the state, regional, and municipal levels and outline a clear path forward. Examples of these strategies include ProsperityNOLA in New Orleans, AdvanceKC in Kansas City, Missouri, and the Metro Phoenix Global Investment Plan.[158]

- Local communities should have business retention and expansion programs to support existing companies in their market. The best estimates suggest that as much as 80 percent of net job growth comes from existing businesses in a city or town; nurturing those businesses and helping them expand is likely to have bigger payoffs than focusing on luring new companies.[159]

- Regions should focus on attracting new companies from the United States and abroad through regional economic development organizations with clear strategies by sector, focusing on sectors in which the region can develop competitive scale.[160]

Other priorities should include an active role in workforce development (discussed in more detail below) and investments in public infrastructure—including amenities such as parks, bike paths, theaters, and other community spaces—to improve the attractiveness and competitiveness of the region as a business investment location.[161]

Test, evaluate, and benchmark investment incentive schemes. States and cities continue to offer tax and other incentives to encourage companies to site their job-creating activities in those locations, though the outcomes of such incentives are usually disappointing for the states.[162] Many states, however, are developing a more sophisticated capacity for ensuring that companies deliver the promised benefits. Model approaches should include transparent reporting on the costs to taxpayers, job-creation outcomes, and quality of jobs created in terms of wages and benefits. Deals should include evaluation criteria and withdrawal and reimbursement of incentives if companies fail to deliver on their job-creating promises.[163]

Private sector

Build capacity in investment locations. Decisions to invest in a new city or region, or to expand operations, are a big commitment for companies.

They are in effect a bet on the continued economic viability of that investment location. That means companies have a stake in building the competitiveness of these locations—including through an educated and skilled populace, world-class infrastructure, and a commitment to research and innovation. Harvard Business School has termed such resources the "commons" from which all companies benefit. Business has a central role, working with local governments, educational institutions, and nonprofits, in building these local capacities.[164]

REVERSE THE SLOWDOWN IN ENTREPRENEURSHIP

Small companies remain an important engine of job growth, and the United States needs to reverse the slowdown in new-company formation. The reduction in tax rates for small businesses as part of the December 2017 tax bill is likely to encourage new start-ups, but further steps are needed.

Expand access to capital. The number of community banks in the United States has declined by one-third over the past decade. Historically, community banks have been an important source of funding for new businesses.[165] Disparities also remain in the type of small-business credit or loans available to women, minorities, and people in economically distressed communities.[166] Expanded funding for community-development financial institutions (CDFIs) would be helpful in addressing these capital gaps. CDFIs have proven particularly effective in delivering capital to minority and rural small-business owners. Large banks should also expand their own initiatives. JPMorgan Chase and Wells Fargo have established programs and funded activities that have targeted "CDFIs of color": JPMorgan's Partnerships for Raising Opportunity in Neighborhoods (PRO Neighborhoods) has created diverse collaborations that bring together disparate organizations to implement innovative programs that support housing and small-business opportunities in underserved communities. Wells Fargo has implemented the Diverse Community Capital program, which seeks to invest $75 million into Latino and African American communities to leverage greater small-business lending. Both programs seek to identify minority-serving CDFIs and community lenders to create greater capacity and borrower results.

Revise the Community Reinvestment Act (CRA). This act should do more to encourage banks to make investments that are more concentrated, coordinated, and focused on job creation. Currently, banks can get CRA credit for investing in or lending to entities that create only low-wage jobs that do not offer a path out of poverty. The CRA could be a much more powerful tool to facilitate community development by focusing on the quality of loans (and in particular small-business loans) to the low- to moderate-income community and on the types of jobs these loans create.

Leverage public funds more effectively to increase working capital lending. The Small Business Administration's lending programs can and should help provide start-up capital, but new private capital sources are needed in struggling communities. It is difficult to know the effectiveness of community small-business financing systems without continuously measuring and tracking successes and challenges over time. The Federal Reserve recently recommended that the Consumer Financial Protection Bureau (CFPB) implement section 1071 of the Dodd-Frank Act to collect data from banks on their small-business lending. Local officials and the private sector could create small-business development corporations to attract private venture capital and offer working capital to small companies.[167] Where possible, state and local leaders should strengthen and expand smaller, local banks and credit unions.

Create an immigrant entrepreneur visa. Immigrants remain a noteworthy exception to the decline in new-company formation in the United States. Immigrants are roughly twice as likely as native-born Americans to start a new business; in 2014, 28.5 percent of new start-ups were founded by immigrants, up from just 13 percent in 1997, and one-quarter of new engineering and technology start-ups had an immigrant founder.[168] Congress should pass legislation that permits immigrants, many of whom are recent graduates from U.S. universities, to live and work in the United States if they can raise funds to start new companies. Among the proposals that have significant bipartisan support is the Startup Act, which would create an entrepreneurial visa to permit seventy-five thousand immigrants annually to remain temporarily in the country if they have raised enough seed capital to launch a new company, and to remain permanently if the company succeeds.[169] Such a visa could add 1.6 million U.S. jobs over the next decade.[170]

Maintain U.S. Technological Leadership

The United States needs to remain a world leader in technology and innovation. This should be supported through increased public and private R&D, support for commercialization of new research, an open door to highly skilled immigrants, and steps to prevent the forced transfer of U.S.-developed technologies to competitors.

If the history of the modern global economy has taught any lesson, it is that those who hesitate to embrace and encourage new technologies will get left behind. The United States is facing growing competition for leadership in innovation, investment, and technology from countries with different economic models. For instance, the Chinese government's direct role in shaping industrial policy and steering companies with financing and other government support contrasts with the U.S. model of open innovation and relaxed regulation. The global race to develop, own, finance, dominate, and disseminate artificial intelligence and other emerging technologies will permeate the business competition of the future and further divide nations based on their ability to capture these gains in a competitive global landscape. Talent is critical—the United States needs to develop or attract the scientists, engineers, and creative talent to lead in this competition. China's drive to dominate these technologies of the future, including big data, quantum computing, artificial intelligence, and autonomous systems, is an economic, educational, and strategic challenge to the United States.

Increase support for basic research. While total R&D spending has been rising in the United States, the share devoted to basic research—which comes mostly from federal support—has been falling, from roughly 1.2 percent of GDP in the 1970s to less than 0.8 percent today.[171] President Trump's proposed 2019 budget would hold the line on research spending (though the administration had proposed deep reductions before the February 2018 congressional budget deal that increased spending caps). The administration is, however, pushing for deeper cuts in such critical areas as renewable energy research.[172] This comes at a time when other countries, including Brazil, China, Singapore, and South Korea, have been increasing their investments sharply. The federal government needs to continue to be a driver of basic research, particularly as development of artificial intelligence becomes a competitive race with nations such as China, which has massively increased its research funding. China has overtaken the United States, for example, in the volume of published journal articles on deep learning.[173] While AI developers can often attract venture capital investors, basic science research is still needed, and the government is best placed to fund it. Government-funded research tends to encourage rather than discourage private-sector R&D, which is far more focused on the development of marketable new products than on advancing the underlying science.[174] And government R&D spending also has the strength of being spread widely around research universities across the country, which can help spur local economic development efforts. The U.S. government should set and meet a target of investing at least 1 percent of GDP in R&D activities.

Maintain the permanent tax incentive for private-sector R&D. The United States was the first country to establish an R&D tax credit, in 1981, and it has proven to be one of the most effective federal tax incentives. It addresses a basic market failure—companies that invest in research do not reap the full benefits of their investment, even though the broader social benefits are enormous.[175] In recent years other nations have adopted similar or greater incentives, so the United States no longer enjoys a significant edge. The December 2017 tax bill maintained the credit but will diminish its benefit by requiring companies to write off the costs of R&D investments over five or more years instead of in a single year. Congress should now assess what significant incentives remain for commercial investment and determine whether additional measures might be beneficial from a competitive standpoint.

Encourage regional and sectoral partnerships in developing and commercializing new research. Such targeted partnerships have proven effective in moving research from the laboratory to production and in establishing successful technology clusters. Manufacturing USA (formerly the National Network for Manufacturing Innovation), for example, which involves the Departments of Commerce, Defense, and Energy, has set up a series of public-private partnerships aimed at the commercialization of new manufacturing technologies, modeled after the German Fraunhofer Institutes. Nine new centers have been launched that cover additive and digital manufacturing, lightweight and composite materials, next-generation integrated circuits, and advanced fabrics.[176] Congress should expand support for this initiative to fund the completion of the fifteen centers originally planned when the program was launched in 2012.[177]

Maintain Small Business Innovation Research (SBIR) funding. The SBIR program, created under President Ronald Reagan in 1982, has been highly successful at encouraging innovative start-ups at modest cost to taxpayers.[178] The program awards roughly $2.5 billion in competitive grants each year to small companies that have shown promising research breakthroughs but have not yet developed the track record to attract venture capital. Apple, Compaq, and Intel are among the companies that received SBIR grants in the 1980s.[179]

Open doors to more highly educated immigrants. Highly skilled immigrants help the U.S. economy. Immigrants are significantly more likely to participate in scientific research leading to patents and to found new companies. U.S. openness to immigration has been a significant contributor to the U.S. lead in innovation.[180] The United States needs to increase its openness to high-skilled immigration, and in particular make it as easy as possible for graduates of U.S. universities in scientific and technical fields to remain and work in the United States. Congress has considered, but not approved, legislation that would give priority to highly educated immigrants, especially foreign students who graduate from U.S. universities, and passing such measures should be a top priority.[181] The administration should also reconsider measures that have created new obstacles for many foreign students and foreign workers on temporary work visas such as the H-1B.[182] Allowing companies to bring talented employees to the United States reduces the incentive to move research and other corporate activities offshore. Steps should also be taken to link immigration more directly with U.S. labor market challenges; Microsoft, for example, has proposed that companies should pay higher fees for H-1B applications, provided the funds are reinvested in U.S. computer science education.[183]

Prevent forced technology transfers. The United States should work with its allies to stop the forced transfer of technologies to foreign competitors. The problem is particularly acute with respect to China, which often demands that foreign investors share proprietary technologies with Chinese competitors as a condition for investing and expanding in the larger Chinese market in sectors such as automobiles, chemicals, and renewable energy. In automobiles, for example, foreign companies are required to manufacture only through joint ventures, and General Motors was required to share the intellectual property of the Chevrolet Volt in order to qualify for subsidies for electric car purchases. Under the Made in China 2025 plan, China is seeking to supplant imports with domestic production in ten advanced-technology sectors, including semiconductors, aircraft, electric cars, and 5G mobile telecommunications.[184] The Trump administration has targeted aspects of the problem through an investigation under section 301 of the Trade Act of 1974. The United States should work with allies in Japan, Europe, and elsewhere that are similarly harmed by Chinese practices. The issue should also be addressed through bilateral investment negotiations and regional and multilateral forums.

State and local governments

Promote innovation clusters. Cities and states need to build on their economic strengths by promoting innovation in sectors where they enjoy local advantages, including universities and other institutions conducting relevant research, a workforce with skills in specific areas, and a cluster of suppliers. The goal of this approach is to identify and leverage the economic strengths of a city or region.[185] The Global Cities Initiative, a project of the Brookings Institution and JPMorgan Chase, has been a leader in identifying best practices for urban and regional economic planners and helping regions build on their strengths to succeed in the global economy.[186]

Private sector

Choose the United States for research and innovation. The United States offers companies enormous benefits for locating their R&D in the United States, including top scientific and engineering talent, a high level of intellectual property protection, and generous tax write-offs. Given the challenges that many companies are facing in protecting intellectual property offshore, companies should look to locate their R&D activities in the United States to the maximum extent feasible.[187]

Boost Growth and Income

Governments at all levels should develop and implement policies aimed at maintaining strong growth and demand for labor. Employers should commit themselves to creating a "high-road workplace" that offers employees decent pay, training, scheduling, and benefits. Special measures are needed for communities struggling to attract investment and jobs.

Federal government

Set the conditions to maintain full employment. The best way to generate and sustain wage growth is to have an economy in which employees are in high demand and employers face pressure to bid up wages in response. Congress should preserve the Federal Reserve's dual mandate of maintaining the maximum sustainable employment and stabilizing prices, and resist calls to target low inflation without concern for employment levels. Congress and the Trump administration should also use fiscal policy prudently to maintain strong growth and employment.

Pass and implement a Make Work Pay tax credit. The Earned Income Tax Credit, created by President Gerald Ford in 1975 and expanded under President Bill Clinton in 1993, provides a refundable tax credit to low-income working individuals. It has been one of the most effective anti-poverty programs in the country and is aimed directly at low-income workers. In 2016, a family with an income of less than $50,000 could claim a refundable tax credit of up to $6,300. Roughly ten million Americans are lifted out of poverty each year by the combination of the EITC and the Child Tax Credit.

The credit should be rebranded and updated for the challenges that exist in the current labor market. It should be renamed the Make Work Pay tax credit, to make it clear that its goal is to help rebuild the link between work and economic security. Several proposals have been made to expand and improve the EITC, which could be fashioned into a new Make Work Pay incentive. First, the credit is currently paid out in a lump sum each year at the time of tax filing, which is less beneficial for individuals and families struggling to make ends meet on a monthly basis. It could easily be modified to pay out on a quarterly or even more regular basis.[188] Other ideas include expanding the EITC to childless adults and increasing the payout significantly to do more to offset low wages.[189]

Expand the national service program. Young people remain among the most economically vulnerable populations; the youth unemployment rate is 9 percent, roughly double the national average. This is one problem that state and local governments, working with nonprofit groups, should tackle directly through expanded service opportunities. Civilian services should be targeted at specific public needs, such as tutoring students from disadvantaged backgrounds, helping the elderly, or working on outdoor projects such as building or maintaining parks and other public spaces. Expanded service programs could also help bridge some of the deep social and political divisions in the United States by allowing young people to work directly with those from different backgrounds. The positions should include modest stipends and preferred access to educational financing after completion of service. Two existing service programs, the Peace Corps and AmeriCorps, currently enroll roughly eighty thousand young people annually. General Stanley McChrystal, who has become a strong advocate for national service, suggests a target of one million new annual positions.[190] Those service programs should also focus on training young people in skills that will have future job-market value. The programs would not be particularly expensive; the Aspen Institute estimates that total taxpayer costs are currently less than $1.5 billion annually, with a fourfold return on investment in terms of skills for the individuals and broader social benefits. Expanding service to one million positions would cost roughly $20 billion, with commensurately larger gains.[191]

State and local governments

Make targeted minimum wage increases consistent with local conditions. The federal minimum wage has fallen in real terms since the late 1960s, from roughly $11 in current dollars to $7.25, a one-third reduction in earnings. The last increase in the federal minimum was eight years ago. While there are certainly good arguments for raising the federal minimum, the large differences in state and local labor markets around the country argue for leaving these decisions up to state and local governments. Twenty-nine states and the District of Columbia have higher-than-national minimum wages, and about forty municipalities have set their own higher minimums. Many cities, including Buffalo, Los Angeles, New York, San Francisco, Seattle, and Syracuse, have adopted or are moving toward a fifteen-dollar-per-hour minimum. On balance, the evidence suggests that higher minimum wages do push up earnings for the lowest-paid workers, including those who were already making slightly more than the minimum, and do little to dampen employment. It also makes sense to raise the minimum wage in conjunction with an expansion of the Make Work Pay credit in order to limit the cost of the subsidy.[192]

The wage level clearly makes a difference; there is some evidence in Seattle—which has already increased its minimum to thirteen dollars an hour—that employers have reduced hours and delayed hiring, though more data are still needed.[193] State and local governments should be left to experiment and adjust to find the optimum level. Too little is known about the effect of higher minimums on employment, especially for younger workers.

Establish Make Work Pay credits. Some twenty-nine states and the District of Columbia currently have their own tax credits for low-income working people, and most are administratively simple because they are set as a percentage of the federal EITC. Many of the states without an EITC are among the poorest in the country, where the benefits would be greatest. Every state should move to adopt some similar tax credit for low-income workers. City and county governments could also offer credits. A pilot project in Atlanta and New York, which increased the credit to $2,000 at tax time, showed that employment rates rose for individuals—especially women—who received the bonus.[194]

States and cities should also experiment with quarterly payouts. Chicago in 2014 pilot tested a program to provide more than two hundred EITC recipients with quarterly payouts based on their expected end-of-tax-year refund. The participating households reported considerable improvements in their household financial stability, including less reliance on credit cards and payday loans and greater ability to save some of the end-of-year refund rather than use it to pay overdue bills.[195]

Private sector

Commit to high-road strategies. Employers are increasingly discovering that a high-road workforce strategy—including decent pay, employment benefits, predictable scheduling, and opportunities for training and advancement—can produce better returns and a more loyal, productive workforce than do strategies focused solely on cost savings.[196] While the opportunities will differ from sector to sector, employers would be wise to get ahead of this curve by taking steps to make themselves more attractive places to work and doing more to support the careers of their employees. BlackRock, the $6 trillion investment fund that is one of the largest in the world, is demanding that each company it holds in its portfolio "not only deliver financial performance, but also show how it makes a positive contribution to society." In his recent letter to CEOs, BlackRock Chairman and CEO Laurence Fink wrote: "We see many governments failing to prepare for the future, on issues ranging from retirement and infrastructure to automation and worker retraining. As a result, society increasingly is turning to the private sector and asking that companies respond to broader societal challenges."[197]

One initiative that has been passed into legislation by thirty-three states encourages willing companies to reorganize as benefit corporations (B Corps), meaning they commit to pursuing general benefits such as responsible workplace practices, community growth, and environmental stewardship in addition to return to shareholders.[198] Governments should look for other ways to encourage, recognize, and reward companies that follow high-road strategies.

ENCOURAGE INVESTMENT IN DISTRESSED COMMUNITIES

Employment opportunities in the United States have become increasingly unequal geographically. The big cities, largely along the coasts, are growing more prosperous, while smaller cities and towns in the heartland of the country face diminishing job prospects. Fifty-two million Americans, some 17 percent of the population, live in "distressed communities" in which sizeable percentages of the population have not finished high school, are absent from the workforce, and face a diminishing number of job opportunities.[199] The highest concentration of these communities is in the South and Midwest, though there are pockets across the country.

Regional disparities seem to be a feature of the two drivers of the modern economy—technology and globalization—both of which reward concentration in the larger urban areas, with their access to highly educated and skilled employees and good connections to global markets.[200] The United States and other countries have pursued a range of policies—from direct corporate subsidies to tax incentives to the creation of enterprise zones (EZs)—to encourage investment in these regions, with mixed success. Most states and many city governments have established economic development organizations whose primary goal is to attract job-creating investments. Australia and Canada have pioneered a model that encourages new immigrants to locate outside their three major cities in order to bring new human capital to places that need it most.[201]

Bringing more investment and job creation to distressed communities is going to require attention to the broader set of recommendations in this report—in particular education and skills training, at local universities (where present) and community colleges working in close conjunction with local employers. But there are specific initiatives that could help.

Expand, revitalize, and reinvest in broadband access. The ability to access advanced telecommunications, including high-quality voice, data, graphics, and video, is becoming the standard entry point for the digital world. In 2016, the Federal Communications Commission (FCC) issued a report on broadband access and found that thirty-four million Americans lacked access to high-speed broadband, a majority of whom live in rural areas or tribal lands. More strikingly, nearly 41 percent of schools, representing 47 percent of American students, lack high-speed connectivity to meet the FCC's benchmark of "connectivity capable of supporting digital learning applications."[202] It is difficult to envision bringing lucrative technology jobs to middle parts of the country if these areas lack reliable broadband access. It will be impossible to use the power of the internet to help workers build skills through digital platforms and online training programs if dial-up is their only connection to the web. It is costly for the private sector to provide access to sparse rural populations or other areas with depressed consumer demand. The FCC should continue to support private deployment through the Connect America, Mobility, and Tribal Mobility funds. The FCC should also maintain a minimum speed requirement for companies to qualify for Connect America support and continue to support discounted broadband access to vulnerable populations through the Lifeline program.

Such initiatives do not need to emanate from Washington alone. Chattanooga, Tennessee, for example, used its own municipally owned electricity company to roll out broadband connections with a speed of one gigabit per second, about fifty times the U.S. average. That has attracted billions of dollars in new investment and young entrepreneurs, helping to continue the revitalization of what had been a struggling industrial city.[203] Federal regulators should encourage similarly ambitious experiments in other cities and towns.

Federal government

Create new enterprise zones. The creation of federal enterprise zones to encourage investment in distressed communities, especially in the inner cities, was a 1990s initiative championed most vocally by the late Jack Kemp, the Republican housing secretary under President George H.W. Bush. The federal government in the 1990s initiated various EZ schemes that offered tax credits tied to the employment of local residents in these communities. While not sufficiently studied, these initiatives may have paid significant returns in terms of higher employment levels and stable or rising housing prices.[204] Critics have argued, however, that the idea was never fully embraced and that the evidence on effectiveness is varied.[205] In the 2017 tax bill, Congress approved a new national community investment program known as Opportunity Zones, which offers tax benefits to encourage long-term investment in low-income urban and rural communities.[206] The program could free up significant investment capital, and its effects should be closely monitored to ensure that funds are going into projects that generate significant economic value in struggling communities.[207]

Authorize state-based immigrant visas. Immigrants can be an important source of new economic demand and entrepreneurial energy in places suffering from slow economic growth. But absent other incentives, new immigrants will tend to follow employment opportunities, which are clustered in the largest cities. In the late 1990s, Canada launched its Provincial Nominee Program in an effort to encourage migrants to spread out beyond the three main cities—Montreal, Ottawa, and Toronto. Provinces are allowed to select immigrants directly—consistent with federal priorities and admissions criteria—to prioritize those with education and skills aligned with local economic needs. Australia has a similar program. The evidence suggests these immigrants have been more economically successful than federally sponsored migrants.[208] Michigan has been advocating changes to U.S. immigration law that would permit similar state nomination of migrants.[209]

State and local governments

Build on existing skills and capacities. Many of the hardest-hit regions in the country depended heavily on the old industrial economy, but it is possible to build on that legacy. Akron, Ohio, for example, has built on its legacy as the tire-making capital of the country to become a leader in polymers. Even with the decline of the tire industry, Akron had a wealth of trained scientists and engineers working with rubber, synthetics, and steel. The University of Akron established the College of Polymer Science and Polymer Engineering, which has become a world leader in the application of polymers for the auto, aerospace, and defense industries and spun off an array of local commercial start-ups.[210] Health and medical research has been an engine of growth in places like Buffalo, Cleveland, and Pittsburgh. North Carolina has made similar strides with modern synthetic fabrics, building on the legacy of its textile and apparel industries.

Attract recent college graduates through low-cost housing. The low cost of housing in many of the older or smaller industrial cities and towns is potentially a magnet for recent college graduates looking to get settled and start families. Many of these places also have potentially valuable old industrial properties that can be refurbished and repurposed. Federal initiatives could help by, for example, offering some student-loan forgiveness to young people who locate in these communities.

Strengthen the Link
Between Education and Work

The United States should set and meet a goal of bringing postsecondary education within the reach of all Americans and linking education more closely to employment outcomes.

Much as high school education became the benchmark for success in the early twentieth century, postsecondary education should be the benchmark for the twenty-first century. But success will not simply mean increasing the numbers of students entering and completing two- or four-year college programs, though that is important. Instead, the goal should be to link educational offerings more closely with employment outcomes, in particular by expanding apprenticeships, work-study programs, and internships to strengthen the link between education and work. New initiatives are also needed to improve affordability and access to postsecondary education, and to encourage lifelong learning.

The efforts should be led primarily by business and educators, mainly at state and local levels. There is no one-size-fits-all solution to the challenge of better linking education and the labor market, and there is room for experimentation involving companies, educators, nonprofits, and state and local governments. Systematic organized efforts are needed, however, to share what is being learned and to scale up successful smaller-scale initiatives.

A society-wide effort is also needed to increase public respect for and acceptance of work-based training programs. While just over

30 percent of Americans ever complete a four-year degree, the default assumption among many parents and educators, reinforced by the media, is that going to a traditional college is the only acceptable path to a good career. As a result, many young Americans overlook the multiple available, and far more affordable, paths to acquiring the education and training needed for well-paying jobs. The country needs to work to remove the assumption that a four-year college degree or beyond is the only path to employment success, and to overcome the stigma that too often dissuades young people from making other educational choices.

Language matters here: the use of the phrase "middle skills" to describe many of these jobs explicitly places them below the "high-skill" jobs that are supposedly available only to graduates of four-year programs. That is misleading, because many of these jobs involve complex abilities to work with computers and other machines and may pay much better than some other supposedly high-skill jobs. Companies, educators, and political leaders should be talking about these as skilled, technical jobs that can require learning and "upskilling" throughout a career.

Such language also reinforces the notion of binary educational and career choices. Many young people who begin work in a technical field after an apprenticeship or work-study program may well wish (and should be encouraged) to return to school to finish four-year or more advanced degrees as their careers progress. Stacked credentials and other innovations that allow individuals to upgrade their education over time and while working can also help.

Develop talent pipelines. Employers, including many small- and medium-sized firms, need a strategy for filling their talent needs. The record number of job openings and persistent complaints among employers about skills shortages are part of a growing body of evidence that employers need to change their strategy—instead of sitting back and hoping that schools will graduate employees with the skills they need, or that they can poach them from other companies, they need to work proactively to develop the talent they need. That means working with local and state governments, and with community colleges and other educational institutions. It also means working with other employers within a particular sector, collaborating to build talent within a sector even as companies compete for that talent. Employers are starting to take this issue far more seriously. In addition to individual company initiatives, the Business Roundtable—the national umbrella group of chief executives—has launched the National Network of Business and Industry Associations to provide impetus for new models of work-study and hiring.[211]

Employers seeking to build the best workforce should also keep in mind that reaching nontraditional employees requires significant outreach and recruitment. Plans to recruit women and minorities, for example, should not be an afterthought once programs and staff are in place. Employers need to be willing to hire knowledgeable, diverse, and well-connected recruiters with ties to local communities, schools, and civic organizations; this should be a priority for company management. There is growing evidence that diverse and inclusive workplaces are a source of competitive advantage for companies.[212]

Expand apprenticeships and other work-study initiatives. American companies are increasingly coming to recognize—later, unfortunately, than competitors in Germany, Japan, Switzerland, and other countries—that nurturing a properly skilled workforce is central to their competitive success. That means that companies need to invest in developing and training the employees they want at early stages and throughout their careers. Apprenticeship models, which can be adapted to many different sectors and skills, involve a mixture of formal education and work-based learning.[213] In Germany, Switzerland, and some other European countries, apprenticeships are an expected and ordinary path into the workforce and do not preclude or discourage students from returning to higher education. They also offer a far more secure path to employment for young people. Good corporate models are already in operation that U.S. companies should examine. German and Swiss companies investing in the United States have been able to bring with them their apprenticeship and workforce training models. BMW in South Carolina, Brose in Michigan, and Volkswagen in Tennessee are among the German companies that have established apprentice programs, working in close association with local German chambers of commerce that bring together other employers. The best models are open models, like the ones established by Toyota, that allow participation by other employers that are willing to offer apprenticeships.

Expanding the scale and benefit of apprenticeships will also require broader industry leadership and adequate attention to address the particular needs of local labor markets. Industry associations such as local chambers of commerce are ideally placed to bring together multiple employers; local workforce development boards should also play a more active role (and are encouraged to do so under WIOA).[214] In traditional apprentice fields such as the building trades, companies should work closely with labor unions that have historically led such training for their members.[215] The model should be a system with multiple options and pathways for students. The intention is not to track students but to open up new possibilities for both education and work.[216]

Improve quality and transparency with respect to industry credentials. There is often great uncertainty over the relationship between the credentials students earn and the employment prospects for graduates with those credentials. Transparency initiatives such as Credential Engine are designed to provide greater transparency and consistency, to allow students, educational institutions, and employers to do a better job of aligning credentialing with workplace opportunities.[217] Many sectors, such as retail, have no standard credentialing system in place at all, which makes it difficult for employees to move freely within the sector. Improvements in credential quality and transparency will also feed back into young people's educational choices, which will in turn help companies develop the talent pipelines they need.

State and local governments

Undertake detailed skills assessments of the population and the workforce needs of local employers. State and local governments need stronger analysis of the education and skills levels of their populations. Devising and implementing appropriate educational options depends on a solid assessment of the workforce needs of local employers and the education and skills level of the state workforce. Policymakers should identify and focus their efforts on priority sectors that offer the likelihood of expanded employment in well-paying jobs.[218]

Work closely with large employers and educational institutions on skills-pipeline initiatives, including expansion of apprenticeships and other work-study experiences. While some large employers have the capacity to work directly with educational institutions to build the talent pipelines they need, success in workforce development generally requires close collaboration among state governments, educational institutions, and employers. States should not simply wait for employers to act but should take the lead in fostering such partnerships. In Colorado, for example, the state's CareerWise Colorado initiative— a partnership involving the state, employers, industry associations, community colleges, public schools, and private foundation funders— launched in 2017 and aims to place twenty thousand students in apprenticeships by 2027. Modeled loosely after the Swiss apprenticeship system, the program is focused on linking education and workplace training in fields including information technology, advanced manufacturing, financial services, and hospitality. It begins in the junior year of high school and runs for three years of combined work and study; at the end, students graduate with an industry-recognized credential, no debt, and, likely, a job offer, as well as a year of college credit that can be transferred to a four-year program.[219]

There are numerous different state models for expanding education-to-work initiatives. The Pathways to Prosperity Network, which was launched in 2011 by the nonprofit Jobs for the Future and Harvard University's Graduate School of Education, is currently operating in fourteen states. Beginning in middle and high schools, the initiative offers early and sustained career counseling to students and workplace-learning opportunities with employers.[220] Many of the skills that lead to success in the workforce are not taught in a classroom but learned while actually doing work.

Connecticut and Iowa offer grants to employers, industry associations, and labor-management partnerships to expand programs; California directs its funds to educational institutions; and South Carolina has a more comprehensive model that includes an employer tax credit of up to $1,000 per apprentice, consultants for employers wanting to establish or expand apprenticeship programs, and close cooperation with the state's technical colleges.[221]

Help small- and medium-sized companies in particular. Smaller companies face challenges in working with governments and educational institutions to meet their workforce needs. This is an area where state and local government involvement can be particularly helpful. Again, Colorado has been a leader here. The state, working with the Markle Foundation's Skillful initiative, LinkedIn, and Microsoft, developed a partnership with employers, educators, and the public workforce development system to help steer students into relevant training programs and to encourage employers to expand their talent pool. The goal is to give educators and students a clearer idea of which skills are in demand, and give smaller employers in particular better access to those skilled workers. In February 2018, twenty U.S. governors announced their collaboration on the Skillful State Network, marking the national expansion of this initiative.[222] The Incentives for Industry Credentials pilot in Colorado, which has the goal of preparing students for jobs in health care, information technology, and advanced manufacturing, also offers a $1,000 bonus to schools when students receive an industry credential tied to an in-demand job or complete a workplace training program.[223]

Expand career counseling in high schools, community colleges, and universities. More and better career counseling—starting in high school or even earlier—is going to be a critical component of preparing young Americans for the jobs of the future. Guidance counselors will need to be aware of the full range of potential employment options for students, including different apprentice and work-study opportunities and community college offerings, as well as university entrance requirements.

Developing online platforms like Journeys, based out of San Diego, should help in this regard and would be strengthened by better access to outcomes data, as discussed below. Companies can also do more to make young people aware of career opportunities. Manufacturing Day, for example, is an initiative of the federal Commerce Department in partnership with companies designed to build local interest in advanced manufacturing careers among middle and high school students. In early October each year, employers open their factory floors and invite local students and educators to visit, test, and learn about modern manufacturing. Igniting interest at an early age, even as young as ten, can help students understand how their studies can directly lead to good jobs later.[224]

Academic guidance is especially important for community college students. As Harry Holzer and Sandy Baum argue, without such guidance, "students can meander aimlessly through courses and fields without purpose or direction, and this can be very costly to students in two-year programs." Given the enormous difference in labor market outcomes between focused programs leading to recognized credentials in high-demand fields and general studies programs, better counseling is especially important for community college students.[225]

Adopt workplace readiness standards as part of middle and high school curricula. While many relevant workplace skills are learned in community colleges and beyond, waiting until students reach that level is simply too late. Few states currently have standards that are tied in any clear way to workforce readiness. These workforce readiness standards fall into two categories: skills readiness standards and capacity standards. Skills readiness standards would be aligned with skills that are or will be in demand for quality jobs in the future or present. These should change over time and be continually revisited by standard setters. Examples of using such standards include the current push toward universal computer science education in K-12.[226] Capacity standards would be aligned with habits of mind required for students to be successful in the workplace. Many of these are already embedded explicitly in other standards in math and reading, but they need to be highlighted and consistently assessed to relate directly and currently to people of different backgrounds and cultures. These capacities are timeless and allow students to more easily adapt to different workplace opportunities.

Create lifelong learning accounts. Most financial assistance for students is aimed at young people seeking education prior to starting careers. Ideally, companies should be funding the bulk of mid-career retraining, as AT&T and some others are doing, but many companies will be reluctant to make these investments. Because the benefits also accrue to the employee in terms of higher salaries and prospects for new jobs, it is reasonable that employees bear some of the burden. Maine was the first state to pilot lifelong learning accounts, in conjunction with the Chicago-based nonprofit Council for Adult and Experiential Learning; Washington State has created similar accounts. In such accounts, employers agree to match the savings their employees put into individual savings accounts, which can then be used for future education.[227] The accounts are portable, allowing employees to take the accrued savings with them if they change jobs. A federal approach, as discussed below, would increase the reach of these accounts significantly.

Regularly update and modernize workforce development legislation and regulations. WIOA, passed by Congress on a bipartisan basis, made a number of improvements to workforce training, including requiring better coordination at state and local levels, encouraging a more active role for employers, and updating performance and accountability requirements. But WIOA was passed sixteen years after the previous iteration of the act. Given the rapid changes in technology and workplace needs, federal workforce systems need far more regular updating.

Focus and increase resources in a transparent fashion. Federal and state funding for community colleges and public universities is simply not keeping pace with the need or the demand. Real spending has fallen by roughly $9 billion, or an average of 16 percent per student, over the past decade; tuition has risen steeply at most institutions to try to cover the costs.[228] Community colleges, which are especially important in opening advanced educational opportunities to lower-income Americans, should be a particular priority. The funding should be focused on improving completion rates for students, which will likely require more resources devoted to academic and career counseling.[229] Private for-profit colleges will continue to play an important role but should be carefully regulated to protect students against aggressive marketing. The impending reauthorization of the Higher Education Act, last reauthorized in 2008, offers an excellent opportunity to tackle many of these issues on a bipartisan basis.

Expand financing options for mid-career retraining, including lifelong learning accounts. The federal government should follow the lead of some states and create a national program to help finance mid-career retraining. Federal participation would amplify such schemes by, for example, allowing individuals to make tax-free contributions to the plans (as with retirement accounts) and offering tax credits to employers for their contributions. The tax benefits should be weighted toward lower-income workers who face greater challenges in saving; Washington could also consider direct contributions to lower-income employees, following examples in France, Singapore, and other countries.[230] An additional or alternative approach would include lifetime career loans that would allow workers to borrow for education and training throughout their careers, with the loans repayable on an income-contingent basis tied to future earnings.[231] The focus here should be on shorter-term training programs. Many mid-career workers are not in a financial position to earn a two-year degree; expansion of stackable credentials and nano-degrees is one encouraging approach, allowing individuals to continue working while earning credentials and building on those credentials over time.[232]

Allow more flexible forms of financing for career-oriented educational programs. Pell Grants are the biggest federal source of student financing, but the support is currently unavailable for most career-focused education and short-term programs. Currently, loans are only available for programs that run for at least fifteen weeks, disqualifying many short-term skills-based training programs. Bipartisan legislation has been introduced that would help fill this gap and support emerging industry-education partnerships, and should be included in the Higher Education Act reauthorization.[233]

Expand federal apprenticeship programs and implement visa reforms to encourage apprenticeship sharing. President Trump's goal of doubling the number of registered apprenticeships is a good place to start, though the administration favors other cuts to training programs. The apprenticeship initiative builds on similar efforts from the end of the Obama administration that provided a boost in funding; the Trump administration has proposed $200 million in funding for fiscal year 2019.[234] Specific visa reforms would also help in bringing European best practices to the United States. European and other foreign-owned companies have been among the leaders in bringing their apprenticeship models to the United States, but U.S. immigration restrictions prevent these firms from bringing apprenticeship trainers to the United States for all but short stints. Changes to immigration law or regulations to expand exchange programs for apprenticeships would help address this barrier.

MAKE BETTER USE OF LABOR MARKET DATA

The Task Force recommends a large-scale effort to improve gathering and disseminating data on labor market needs, trends, and outcomes. Unleashing the full potential of labor market data though the creation of an open public-private data infrastructure would do an enormous amount to empower students and employees and reduce labor market frictions.

The growth in data about the labor market has been enormous and will only accelerate. Harnessing that wealth of data to produce better outcomes should be a top priority of governments, employers, and educational institutions. While the federal government in particular continues to be a critical source of labor market information through its annual randomized surveys, a growing portion of the data is now in the hands of the private sector, including companies such as Burning Glass, Indeed, LinkedIn, and Monster. The goal should be to link this disparate data—which include demographics, job openings, credential and experience requirements, education levels, wages, and other relevant information—and make it widely available to researchers and application developers. It should become increasingly possible to follow with precision individual education and career pathways and allow individuals and employers to make better choices. The aim should be to create a data ecosystem that can be used to improve employment outcomes for Americans.

Federal government

Preserve and expand government survey data. These include the American Community Survey and the Current Population Survey. While private-sector data offer a powerful new tool for understanding the labor market, they will never replace the large-scale surveys produced by the federal government. Those surveys, however, have been undermined by the public's declining rate of response to mail and phone surveys.[235] The government needs to revitalize its survey methodology, which will require a boost in resources.

Partner with private companies to enhance the accuracy and utility of labor market data. Government survey data remain extremely valuable to researchers, policymakers, and educators, but as the job market grows more complex and the hiring needs of companies more specific, general survey data have become less useful in helping identify and respond to skills shortages. The federal government should partner with companies that are harnessing labor market data to ensure the timeliest updating and release of relevant labor market information.

Develop an open, shareable national standard for online job postings. Online job postings have not yet begun to reach their potential as a reliable and timely signal for real-time labor market information. For that goal to be realized, the United States needs open, consistent standards for hiring announcements that would make the information easy to access and query, and easy for third-party providers to share through targeted applications. Achieving this goal will require close cooperation among the federal government, employers, and companies that offer online job listings or aggregate labor market data.[236] The National Institute of Standards and Technology (NIST) should be tasked with working with private-sector partners to create these standards.

Promote transparency and accountability in educational institutions. The Obama administration advocated strongly for greater data transparency. It pioneered new efforts to improve accountability from universities and colleges that receive federal aid, though it backed away from its more ambitious plan to develop a nationwide rating system for postsecondary institutions.[237] The federal College Scorecard offers students the ability to compare institutions with respect to tuition, graduation rates, starting salaries for graduates, and student debt loads, though it lacks other important data such as job placement rates.[238] Washington should move ahead with additional initiatives to promote transparency and accountability. The bipartisan proposed College Transparency Act, for example, would lift restrictions in current law that limit the use of federal data for tracking and reporting student graduation rates and employment outcomes.[239] It enjoys broad support among educational institutions and should be included in the reauthorization of the Higher Education Act.

State and local governments

Encourage data sharing by the private sector. In the absence of federal leadership, state governments could also take the lead in fostering the sharing of public and private labor market information on a statewide basis. Virginia's Open Data, Open Jobs initiative is an example of one such effort.[240]

Strengthen labor market outcome reporting by colleges and universities. Most community colleges survey students graduating from their CTE programs, but only on a limited basis and generally looking at the earnings in just the first year following graduation. It is expensive for colleges to do the labor market analysis required to assess the likely outcomes for students in certain programs, which may inhibit them from launching new offerings even when there appears to be growing employer demand.[241] States should help expand the reach of these surveys.

Private sector

Share labor market data more broadly to support public policy. Burning Glass, LinkedIn, and other companies have compiled a wealth of data on local job markets, employer demands, skills gaps, and other challenges.[242] These and other data-gathering companies should continue to look for ways to collaborate with educational institutions and governments to share that information as broadly as possible.

Overhaul Transition
Assistance for Workers

Unemployment insurance should be overhauled to reflect the realities of the current economy, and mid-career retraining programs should adopt the best features of the European "flexicurity" models.

While many of the challenges facing the U.S. workforce are shared among all the advanced economies, U.S. performance is especially weak in helping those who lose jobs find their way back into the labor market. Several detailed cross-national studies into these programs have found the United States lagging significantly.[243]

There are three broad models of transition support: the laissez-faire model, with minimal job security and minimal unemployment benefits, in which most of the costs of adjustment fall on individual workers themselves; the job protection model, characterized by high levels of job security and large, unconditional unemployment insurance for those who lose their jobs; and an active labor market, or flexicurity model, which also has minimal job security but is coupled with generous unemployment insurance supplemented by classroom and on-the-job retraining.[244] The first two models—characterized by the United States and France, respectively—have both proven deficient. The U.S. model places too much burden on the individual and leads too many to exit the labor market (through, among other things, SSDI claims). University of Toronto Professor Michael Trebilcock also argues that the laissez-faire model is "politically perverse in intensifying opposition to trade, technology, and other factors affecting the demand for labor in developed economies." The French model, on the other hand, has focused on preserving full-time employment at the expense of part-time workers and the chronically unemployed. France suffers from extremely high youth unemployment, close to 25 percent, and overhauling France's rigid labor market has been the top priority for President Emmanuel Macron.[245]

The advantages of the third model have been demonstrated by the Nordic countries of Denmark, the Netherlands, and Sweden and also increasingly by Germany, following a series of reforms to its labor market policies.[246] The approach provides a robust system for returning employees to the job market.

Federal government

Build on WIOA and expand the available resources. Under WIOA, Congress has championed a long-overdue employer-centered approach to job retraining. However, the federal funds available under WIOA are minimal, and the Trump administration has proposed deeper cuts. Federal funding for adult education has been cut by 20 percent over the past fifteen years, while CTE has been cut by 30 percent and state job-training grants by 40 percent.[247] The United States should invest more heavily in retraining to see successful outcomes, but those expenditures should be evaluated far more closely than in the past to reward initiatives that are successful at returning displaced workers to good jobs. WIOA's focus on accountability and evaluation is an important step forward and should be reinforced. Finally, replacing the TAA program with a broader program that covers displaced workers regardless of the causes of their job loss (except for voluntary quitting or justified dismissals) should be a top federal priority. Implementation, however, should be at the state and local level.

Increase flexibility in unemployment insurance. In most states, UI eligibility rules require displaced workers to be actively seeking full-time employment, which discourages individuals from seeking part-time work or starting their own businesses. Given the growth of nontraditional work and the importance of getting displaced workers back into jobs as quickly as possible, such restrictions should be eased.[248]

Experiment at scale with wage insurance for displaced workers, focusing on older workers who are less likely to be able to retrain for entirely new careers. Workers who lose their jobs are often forced to take new ones at lower levels of pay, and the longer they are out of the labor market the deeper the pay cut is likely to be. An expanded subsidy program could encourage employers to rehire displaced individuals more quickly. Economic research suggests that on-the-job training is often more effective than outside programs, and wage insurance acts as a kind of training subsidy for employers. Wage insurance normally makes up half the lost wages a worker faces for some specified period of time, normally two years.[249] The program has to date been tested on only a small population of older workers eligible for TAA, and its broader efficacy remains unclear; it should be tested on a larger scale for older workers as part of reforms to the UI system.[250] While wage insurance can act as a subsidy allowing employers to hold down wages, it is likely to be offset by the much higher societal costs of long-term unemployment, including increased use of SSDI, which is far more expensive. Because wage insurance and the EITC have similar effects (expanding income for lower-wage workers and keeping them in the labor market), changes to the two programs should be designed in conjunction.

Allow more generous relocation support for displaced workers. Current federal support programs provide little incentive for displaced workers to move to search for new jobs. Under the TAA program, for example, relocation support is capped at just $1,500. Mihir Desai of Harvard Business School has recommended a $15,000 relocation tax credit (rather than a tax deduction) that would begin to phase out for Americans with incomes above $75,000 and for anyone over sixty.[251]

State and local governments

Provide greater career counseling and guidance. Students, families, and employees need advice and guidance to understand how to navigate a rapidly changing employment landscape. Professional counselors provide a macro overview of the job market and can advise workers on the skills needed to make themselves more competitive within their own occupations or for openings in entirely different occupations. Colorado has led the country by hiring new "career navigators" to assist both students and those facing job transitions.[252] The successful reemployment systems in Denmark and Sweden rely heavily on career counselors to advise individuals on the best options for reentering the workforce. Counselors should also help individuals identify skills and experiences they have developed in one industry or sector that may be easily adapted to other sectors.[253] Identifying such skill adjacencies should become more central to retraining efforts.

Private sector

Offer advance notice of layoffs and other significant disruptions. Time is an important asset for employees; sudden layoffs can leave individuals scrambling to cover lost income, acquire additional training, and find new employment. Under the 1988 Worker Adjustment and Retraining Notification Act, companies that employ more than one hundred workers are required to give sixty days' notice in the event of any mass layoffs. All employers should strive to give their employees the longest possible warning in the event of layoffs.

Develop employee skills on the job. Employers should follow the high-road examples discussed above by supporting new educational and training opportunities for their employees, even if those programs are not directly connected to their current jobs. This will make it easier for employees to find new jobs in the event of layoffs and will strengthen the overall capabilities of the U.S. labor force, which is a competitive advantage for the United States.

Remove Barriers
to Opportunity

Governments and employers should work to reduce barriers to labor mobility for Americans, including high housing costs, occupational licensing restrictions, and inflexible hiring practices.

Americans move much less for jobs than they once did, and the decline has been especially steep since 2000. This has limited the historic flexibility of the U.S. labor market, leaving skills shortages in some places and a dearth of work in others. While there are many reasons to think that mobility will never recover to its historic highs—including an aging population and the growth of two-income households—governments should be working actively to address the more easily removable barriers to mobility. Employers can also do far more to improve the hiring process and open opportunities to employees they might otherwise overlook.

State and local governments

Align, recognize, and reduce state occupational licenses. The enormous growth in the number of licensed occupations has shone a light on the incompatibility among state licensing regimes. A massive 2017 national study suggested that the growth of these licensing regimes has stifled competition and opportunity, and in many cases the schemes do not protect consumers against valid health and safety concerns.[254] Once licensed, occupations are rarely delicensed by governments, creating a ratchet effect of greater restrictions.[255] The National Governors Association, in cooperation with the Council of State Governments and the National Conference of State Legislatures, has launched a new effort to improve the portability and reciprocity of occupational licensing across state borders.[256] The project involves eleven states and thirty-four licensed occupations, from barbers to plumbers to real estate agents. The project is scheduled to run for three years from its start in 2017, in recognition of the complexity and political sensitivity of the undertaking. But that timetable is too slow, given the burdens created, and the effort should be accelerated and should include the elimination of unnecessary licensing restrictions.

Support and expand access to affordable housing and job opportunities. The high cost of housing is a considerable deterrent to people moving to the cities that are creating jobs the fastest. Fast-growing cities should pay close attention to the labor market barriers posed by high housing costs. Options for addressing this issue include affordable housing subsidies, lessening of zoning restrictions that discourage high-density development, and improvements in public transit to speed up longer commutes.

Private sector

Reform hiring practices to open opportunities for people without degrees. Employers should have a strong self-interest in expanding their hiring pipeline to ensure they are getting the best talent at the best price. Instead of defaulting to four-year graduates, hiring should focus more effectively on the competencies and experience needed to fill positions, which would bring benefits to both companies and overlooked employees. Initiatives such as Genesys Works, Skills for Chicagoland's Future, Tech Hire, and Year Up offer encouraging models that help create new opportunities for Americans to develop the skills needed for the technology workforce and for employers to find and hire those individuals.[257] Governments should also find ways to support these initiatives through grants and partnerships.

Overhaul Support for Work

> The United States should create portable systems of
> employment benefits tied to individual employees rather
> than to the jobs themselves. Employers should also help
> fill the gap by expanding benefits for their part-time and
> contingent workers.

The Task Force believes that work is important not only for people's
economic success but also for its ability to provide purpose and meaning, self-respect and dignity. However, the dislocations that have
already taken place in the job market, and the potential for far larger
ones to come with the maturing of digital technologies, robotics, and
artificial intelligence, have set off a debate over whether the United
States should pursue policies that delink income from work. The most
far-reaching of these is the idea of paying a universal basic income (UBI)
to all Americans above a certain age. That income would provide a floor
through which no individual or family would fall.[258] The arguments for
UBI cannot and should not be dismissed lightly. One of the reasons for
the proliferation of low-wage work is that too many Americans have
no other choice—if they refused such work, there would be few other
sources of legitimate income. UBI would provide greater security
for workers to pursue occupations that are appealing to them, rather
than simply take jobs out of necessity. That might force employers
to find ways to make work more attractive. UBI also has the great
virtue of bureaucratic simplicity; it requires no complicated analysis of

need but instead involves the government cutting and mailing checks every month, something it does efficiently. This simplicity is one of the features that has united some thinkers on the right and the left behind UBI.[259]

Despite its merits, however, the Task Force does not recommend moving in that direction. The Task Force members believe that both the enormous cost and the potential disincentives to work are strong negatives of UBI. What advocates of UBI do rightly recognize, however, is that the current system in the United States for supporting its workforce is outdated and inadequate. It ties most employment benefits to full-time jobs that are gradually being replaced or augmented by more flexible forms of work, but those flexible work arrangements often come without the basic benefits that are needed to turn precarious work into more secure work.

Federal government

Establish portability of work-based benefits. With the growth of the gig economy, contract work, and people working multiple jobs, the United States needs to move toward delinking benefits (health care, retirement, sick leave, vacation time) from single employers and full-time work. The OECD, the World Economic Forum, and others have argued that the move toward portability of benefits would not only provide a better and more secure safety net for workers but would also allow employers to hire in more flexible ways and permit employees to work in more flexible ways.[260] Correctly designed, a portable system of benefits could unlock significant value for the United States by allowing both employers and employees to organize work in ways that best suit their needs and interests.

Any system of portability should have three essential features. First, the benefits should be tied to the employee and be available as they move from one job to another. Second, the system should be universal in order to eliminate incentives for employers to hire part-time workers to escape the obligation to offer benefits. Third, benefits should be prorated so contributions to a worker's benefits are tied to the hours worked for each employer. A number of countries have been experimenting with these sorts of systems. For example, France's Compte Personnel d'Activité, or personal activity accounts, launched in 2017, is a pilot program in linking occupational benefits directly to the worker rather than the workplace.[261]

Various proposals have been made on how to construct such a

portable benefits scheme in the United States. Nick Hanauer and David Rolf have argued for the creation of what they call shared security accounts as a way to address this challenge.[262] Employers would pay benefits to employees on a prorated basis—for example, an employee with two twenty-hour-per-week jobs would get half benefits from each of her employers. The benefits would accrue in an individual account that would be portable to future jobs as well. The Aspen Institute's Future of Work Initiative has laid out other possible models—none of them mutually exclusive—including multiemployer plans, single industry schemes, and group insurance plans.[263] The question of how contributions should be made, and the share of the burden that should fall on employers versus employees, is obviously challenging with all these schemes.

Senator Mark Warner (D-VA) has introduced legislation to launch a small pilot project that would offer grants for institutions willing to experiment with different approaches. In theory, portable benefits programs could be run by state governments, labor unions, or other nonprofit organizations.[264] Several European countries have instituted prorated benefits for part-time and contract workers, with partial benefits and contributions to retirement adjusted accordingly. In the Netherlands, for example, half of the workforce is currently in some sort of part-time work, a situation that is sustainable in part by the prorating of work-related benefits.[265]

Creating a new benefits system that supports the way Americans actually work today, and the way employers need and wish to hire to maximize their competitive efficiency, is perhaps the most urgent task for the U.S. government today. As the Aspen Institute's Future of Work Initiative report argues: "Right now, we have an unprecedented opportunity to create a new working world, one in which workers have the ability to choose how and when they work, and do not have to sacrifice social insurance to do so."[266]

State and local governments

Experiment with portability pilot projects. State and local governments should pilot portable benefits programs, perhaps starting with their own state and municipal workforces. Lawmakers in several states, including New York and Washington, have considered schemes to establish portable benefits.[267]

Private sector and other employers

Broaden benefits for employees. Any portability scheme should acknowledge that a majority of employers already provide benefits for their employees, such that no remediating government action is necessary. Some employers that require large part-time and flexible workforces—companies as diverse as Costco, REI, Starbucks, UPS, and Whole Foods—already provide most or all workplace benefits for their part-time employees.[268] Starbucks recently announced an expansion of its benefits program to included paid sick leave, time to care for ill family members, and additional maternity or paternity leave.[269] The more employers do on their own to fill this gap, the easier the challenge will be to overcome.

Next Steps:
Launch a National Dialogue
on the Workforce of the Future

> To underscore the urgency of the task of building the workforce of the future, the president and the nation's governors should create a National Commission on the U.S. Workforce to carry out research, share best practices, and conduct public outreach on workforce challenges. This should be the start of an ongoing effort to put workforce issues at the center of the national conversation.

The challenges discussed in this report will confront the United States for many years to come. While some of the recommendations can be implemented quickly, others will take years or even decades to come to full fruition. Just as important as the specific recommendations is the broader need to put these issues—which are critical not just to U.S. domestic prosperity but to the country's future standing in the world—front and center as a national priority.

Federal and state governments

Create a National Commission on the U.S. Workforce. Such a commission would put much greater research and political muscle behind this agenda, going well beyond such existing and helpful initiatives as the National Governors Association Center for Best Practices and the Mayors Business Council of the U.S. Conference of Mayors.[270] The commission should be composed of the secretaries of commerce, defense, education, labor, transportation, and the treasury; the head of the Small Business Administration; the director of the White House National Economic Council; three Democratic and three Republican members of Congress, selected by leadership; six governors, selected through the National Governors Association; and six mayors, selected through the U.S. Conference of Mayors. It should also have representation from business, educational institutions, labor, and the leading nonprofit, youth, and civic groups working on workforce development. The commission should have a full-time research staff sponsor to lead ongoing research on workforce challenges, and it should become a clearinghouse for sharing across the country the best practices currently being adopted by companies, state and local governments, unions, foundations, and others. The commission should issue a Quadrennial Jobs and Workforce Review, similar to those currently being produced in the Departments of Defense and Homeland Security, which would serve as an ongoing evaluation and strategy document detailing progress and offering future strategies for the issues addressed in this report.

Adopt high-profile metrics for assessing and measuring progress. The commission should develop—working with the country's best labor market economists and other experts—a set of publicly compelling measurements for tracking and reporting progress in building the workforce of the future. The most closely tracked measures of economic performance—including GDP and the unemployment and inflation rates—are not especially useful for assessing progress on workforce issues. Three possibilities, not mutually exclusive, include an employability rate, a good jobs index, and a human capital metric. The employability rate or, alternatively, skills deficit index would assess how many Americans have the skills needed to fill the available jobs. The skills deficit index would be the number of workers needed in occupations versus the number who have developed the skills for those positions. The good jobs index would look at the prevalence and growth of good jobs by industry, occupation, and region (with "good jobs" being defined as those that pay a decent, family-supporting wage and offer some combination of benefits). Georgetown University's Center on Education and the Workforce is currently developing such an index, focused only on jobs that do not require a bachelor's degree, as part of its new Good Jobs Project.[271] The human capital measure was developed by the World Bank. The definition of human capital is the estimated present value of the future earnings of a country's labor force. This is broken down into two components: the probability that various individuals will be working, and their likely future earnings. Investment in education, training, and other initiatives that increase the likelihood of employment and higher future earnings would boost a country's human capital index.[272]

Create a new award, modeled after the successful Baldrige Awards, to recognize and promote companies that follow high-road workplace practices. The Baldrige Award, named after the late Secretary of Commerce Malcolm Baldrige, was established by Congress in 1987 to recognize U.S. companies that implemented successful management systems. The award was created in response to the crisis in U.S. competitiveness in the face of rising competition from Japan, to encourage U.S. companies to emulate and surpass the highly effective Japanese quality control and management systems in such sectors as automobiles and consumer electronics (ironically, the Japanese learned much of this from the United States initially).[273] The award is credited with focusing U.S. companies on the ongoing need for quality improvement. In 1990, the *New York Times* called it "a glittering prize for many top executives who see it as an official recognition of their behind-the-scenes efforts to improve quality." IBM Chairman John Akers said the award "helped rally business around a common objective."[274]

A similar award should be created to recognize companies that implement high-road workplace strategies—including ongoing training and education for employees, decent pay, flexibility in scheduling, family-friendly benefits, responsible management of the supply chain, and cooperation with local communities. The goal should be to drive a corporate revolution similar to the one encouraged by the Baldrige Awards.

Establish a crowdsourced challenge to tackle future workforce problems. This challenge should incentivize Americans to generate ideas, create conversations, and develop solutions at the grassroots level on specific problems facing the future workforce. Such a challenge could be modeled after crowdsourced platform challenges such as HeroX, Solve at the Massachusetts Institute of Technology, and Tongal, and should include prizes.[275]

Establish an ongoing public outreach strategy on workforce issues. The commission should hold ongoing, geographically dispersed public hearings to learn from young people at the start of their careers, those in struggling communities, and workers in transition. There should also be advertising campaigns, particularly on social media—enlisting public figures from entertainment, the media, and the sports world— to highlight the available resources and to encourage young people to make the best possible educational-to-work choices.

Cooperate with other countries through the Group of Twenty (G20) and other forums to share best practices. The future of work is one of the three priority items for the 2018 G20 summit in Argentina and is likely to remain high on the agenda for many years to come. The United States should work with other countries to create a mechanism to share best practices internationally. Such cooperation should also be pursued through the International Labor Organization and the OECD, and through NAFTA with respect to continental workforce challenges.[276]

ADDITIONAL AND DISSENTING VIEWS

Let me praise the Task Force co-chairs, directors, and members for producing a report that is clear-eyed and comprehensive in its assessment of the current state of the U.S. workforce. I am proud and humbled to have been a member of this group, and I endorse the report. That said, there are places the report should go further with its recommendations to prepare the U.S. workforce for the new world that is already here.

Create a national floor for workplace readiness standards. The report strongly advocates for workplace readiness standards that would prepare students with the targeted technical skills the job market demands (such as computer programming) and habits of mind that will always be needed (such as communication skills and leadership across difference). However, I depart from the report on this matter because I strongly believe that these standards should be developed nationally—not by each state individually. While I believe there should be regional variation, there needs to be a national floor for workforce readiness in the U.S. educational system so a business knows that wherever it is, students are properly prepared. I believe the National Commission on the U.S. Workforce would be an excellent venue for all stakeholders (public, private, and social sector) to develop these critical standards.

Focus on returning citizens. Thousands of people reenter American society every year following incarceration. They are disproportionately poor and minority and, according to the Brookings Institution, are likely to be rearrested within five years. Helping this population reenter the workforce would enhance both social justice and workforce competitiveness. To do so, the United States should remove many of the regulations and laws that keep returning citizens from getting back into the workforce. For example, many states allow occupational licensing boards and private employers to summarily reject applicants purely because of a criminal history. Barriers like these should be removed and resources should be put into preparing returning citizens for the jobs of the future before they reenter. The Last Mile is a group that teaches prisoners at San Quentin State Prison to code, and Defy Ventures is helping current and formerly incarcerated people become entrepreneurs. Efforts like these should be encouraged, given resources, and replicated across the country.

Increase the national minimum wage. The report calls for targeted minimum-wage increases across the country; I believe that the report should go further and advocate for a higher federal minimum wage across the country. While a minimum-wage increase would not, in and of itself, solve the workforce challenge, it would make a substantial difference to millions of minimum-wage workers across the country.

Pairing these additional recommendations with those already in the report will provide a real road map to creating the workforce that the economy demands and the United States deserves.

—*Chike Aguh*
joined by Cecilia E. Rouse

This report provides a critically important and timely blueprint for building a stronger U.S. workforce. In particular, the findings in the section "Support for Work in the New Economy" highlight the growing challenges faced by some of the most vulnerable Americans—and the corresponding recommendations advance creative policy responses to mitigate the effects of technological changes and alterations in the traditional employer-employee relationship.

I offer four additional points below: the first two to clarify how the report ties into my own perspectives on trade, and the third and fourth to amplify specific findings and recommendations.

Expanded trade and investment can bring significant benefits to a broad cross section of the U.S. workforce. However, experience shows that this is by no means inevitable, and it is therefore essential that policies and programs be crafted carefully to support greater job creation, promote workers' rights at home and abroad, and advance sustainable economic growth.

Trade Adjustment Assistance indeed was, as noted in endnote 106, "part of the political bargain" on trade when it was established in 1962 and over the succeeding half century. That makes it all the more important that the recommendation to eliminate TAA is part of a proposal for a broader and more generous program for displaced workers.

The report's call for employers to "commit themselves to creating a 'high-road workplace'" and for a new leadership award in this area should launch a broader conversation about responsible business conduct—including the role of business in helping address a range of challenges both at home and abroad (particularly today, when government too often fails to fulfill its own responsibilities). The good news is that as more businesses succeed by pursuing these high-road strategies, they will demonstrate what President Obama said in his final State of the Union address: "doing right by their workers or their customers or their communities ends up being good for their shareholders" as well.

Finally, while the report appropriately centers on the challenges facing the U.S. workforce, these challenges, and therefore the roles of government and the private sector, do not stop at the water's edge. Workers around the world face new risks of job loss and other dislocation as a result of automation and changing production methods and sourcing practices; the effect is likely to be greatest for those at the bottom of global supply chains, living where governments often lack the resources (and in some cases the political will) to respond adequately. It is essential that government and business leaders find common ground with those representing labor, civil society, and international institutions to develop and implement innovative policies and programs to address these growing global economic and security challenges.

—*Eric R. Biel*

The United States needs a national innovation investment strategy to maintain global technological leadership. The global economy today is deeply integrated, with borders fungible to technology and competition a constant reality. If the United States does not attract, invest in, and build industries of the future, it will see lower growth, less national wealth, and fewer good jobs.

Historically, the United States has encouraged innovation by building a strong private-sector business environment, relying on laissez-faire capitalism to allocate capital most efficiently, and it has been culturally reluctant to involve government in business. This approach has made the United States the wealthiest country in history.

But the rules of the game are suddenly changing because of the exponential growth of technologies such as artificial intelligence and blockchain. In the long term, markets will always be the most efficient method of allocating capital. But for now, the United States has to compete with nondemocratic countries that deploy vast amounts of targeted investment capital to win new technology industries and define the future. The United States therefore cannot use the same playbook as yesteryear and requires a new national innovation investment framework to win the industries of the future.

The nature of democracies means that decision-making is inclusive and deliberate, but often slow. In an exponentially growing world where every doubling has dramatic implications, the speed of investment and innovation matters—and the countries that can make faster investment allocation decisions will define the future. Laissez-faire innovation will not be able to compete fast enough with other nations' targeted investments and mercantilist policies, such as those in China, Estonia, and the United Arab Emirates.

China is allocating $150 billion in its current five-year plan to build a powerhouse artificial intelligence industry. Soon, the country's facial-recognition capabilities will allow artificial intelligence to identify any citizen within three seconds and with 90 percent accuracy. This is not a result of haphazard market-led innovation, but rather a direct consequence of China's commitment to becoming the world leader in artificial intelligence within ten years. And if it does so, it will exert oversize influence globally, including on the United States.

The United Arab Emirates has committed to migrating every government transaction onto the blockchain by 2020. If successful, Dubai will likely develop global market leadership in this new industry. And Estonia is building the world's most advanced e-government and attracting entrepreneurs from around the world to its digital shores. Neither of these are accidents of innovation; they are sustained and deliberate national innovation investment priorities.

The United States needs a proactive and intentional innovation investment strategy to win future industries. Otherwise, its bottom-up model will be slow to compete with other countries' targeted, top-down innovation priorities. The United States does not need to pick specific winners in an industry or play an activist role in managing the economy, but it does need to develop road maps for critical future industries that will employ many Americans in high-value-added innovation economy jobs.

The United States should pass legislation—the America First Innovation Act—to spur industries of the future by prioritizing investment in them, supporting their growth with regulation, and opening government labs to accelerate their development and private-sector commercialization. U.S. leadership abroad and the future U.S. workforce depend on a new national innovation investment strategy.

—*Kian Gohar*
joined by Chike Aguh

I am proud to endorse this report, with the following reservations:

The report does not sufficiently stress the risks U.S. workforce challenges present to American democracy and global leadership. These risks are palpable and warrant an aggressive, focused effort. Self-determination, quality of life, and opportunity are core values of the United States. Previous generations knew that with adequate education and training, and a diligent work ethic, there were few limits to what they could achieve. This is no longer true. As Americans feel less secure economically, those insecurities play out in protectionist trade policies, anti-immigrant tendencies, and population polarization along racial and geographic lines. The belief in economic opportunity, free trade, and interdependence have historically strengthened the United States and its economy. However, current rhetoric and policy choices suggest a more individualistic, corporatist path that degrades that spirit and weakens U.S. potential. The long-term consequences of this direction challenge the U.S. posture as the world's leading democracy, capitalist mecca, and global moral authority. The erosion of opportunity and the visceral policy backlash create a scenario in which only the very fortunate or privileged can be successful, and social unrest becomes more likely.

The report downplays the role of the federal government's poor investment decisions in our current economic position; these decisions have largely ignored the middle class and made the poor poorer. The federal government's failure to make globally comparable strategic investments in research and infrastructure during the last several decades has aided in the erosion of the United States' global economic position. Achieving full employment requires a mix of human-capacity building, strategic investments in research and infrastructure, and thoughtful trade and tax policy. The federal government has made few strategic long-term investments in these areas, but it must do so to expand opportunity and create capacity, just as local governments must tailor and refine solutions for their local realities. Unfortunately, federal investments in basic research are their lowest since the 1950s, and infrastructure deficiencies represent a $4 trillion GDP loss and $7 trillion loss in U.S. sales, which will result in the loss of 2.5 million American jobs by 2025, according to the American Civil Society of Engineers' 2016 Infrastructure Report Card. Meanwhile, as the private sector increases investments in these areas and foreign governments increase efforts to lure American operations overseas, the outlook is not favorable for U.S. long-term economic competitiveness if national investment trends in the workforce, research, and infrastructure are not reversed.

While the report does acknowledge some racial and geographic disparities, it does not address the undeniable connection between improving outcomes for people of color and boosting the country's competitive position, strengthening the global narrative, and augmenting economic opportunity. Without significant improvement in the social and economic conditions of nonwhite people, prospects for long-term American economic strength are limited. According to demographic trends, people of color will be the majority of the U.S. population by the 2040s, which means the fate of the United States is inexorably linked to the economic realities of nonwhite people, who typically lag behind the general population in nearly every social and economic indicator. Poor outcomes and lack of access to opportunity for people of color will result in a competitive disadvantage for the United States unless these disparities are addressed directly, with specific programs and policies tailored to these communities.

—*Rodrick T. Miller*

ENDNOTES

1. Bureau of Labor Statistics, "Labor Force Statistics From Current Population Survey: Databases, Tables and Calculators by Subject," February 16, 2018, http://data.bls.gov /timeseries/LNS11300000. See also Arne L. Kalleberg and Till M. von Wachter, "The U.S. Labor Market During and After the Great Recession: Continuities and Transformations," *RSF: The Russell Sage Foundation Journal of the Social Sciences* 3, no. 3 (April 2017): 1–19, http://rsfjournal.org/doi/full/10.7758/RSF.2017.3.3.01; Sandra E. Black, Diane Whitmore Schanzenbach, and Audrey Breitwieser, "The Recent Decline in Women's Labor Force Participation," Hamilton Project, October 2017, http:// hamiltonproject.org/assets/files/decline_womens_labor_force_participation_ BlackSchanzenbach.pdf. While labor force participation did fall more steeply during the recession, there has been a reasonably steady decline since 2000 driven by rising retirements and declining work among prime-age men. See Alan B. Krueger, "Where Have All the Workers Gone? An Inquiry Into the Decline in the U.S. Labor Force Participation Rate," Brookings Papers on Economic Activity, September 2017, http:// brookings.edu/bpea-articles/where-have-all-the-workers-gone-an-inquiry-into-the -decline-of-the-u-s-labor-force-participation-rate.

2. Annie Lowrey, "The Great Recession Is Still With Us," *Atlantic*, December 1, 2017, http://theatlantic.com/business/archive/2017/12/great-recession-still-with-us/547268.

3. David Autor, David Dorn, Gordon Hanson, and Kaveh Majlesi, "Importing Political Polarization? The Electoral Consequences of Rising Trade Exposure," December 2017, http://ddorn.net/papers/ADHM-PoliticalPolarization.pdf; Italo Colantone and Piero Stanig, "The Trade Origins of Economic Nationalism: Import Competition and Voting Behavior in Western Europe," January 21, 2017, http://bancaditalia.it/pubblicazioni /altri-atti-seminari/2016/14_novembre_Colantone_Stanig.pdf; Monica Anderson, "6 Key Findings on How Americans See the Rise of Automation," Pew Research Center, October 4, 2017, http://pewresearch.org/fact-tank/2017/10/04/6-key-findings -on-how-americans-see-the-rise-of-automation.

4. Jay Shambaugh et al., *Thirteen Facts About Wage Growth*, Hamilton Project, 2017, http://hamiltonproject.org/assets/files/thirteen_facts_wage_growth.pdf.

5. "A Look at Pay at the Top, the Bottom, and In Between," Bureau of Labor Statistics, May 2015, http://www.bls.gov/spotlight/2015/a-look-at-pay-at-the-top-the-bottom-and-in

-between/pdf/a-look-at-pay-at-the-top-the-bottom-and-in-between.pdf.

6.   Raj Chetty et al., "The Fading American Dream: Trends in Absolute Income Mobility Since 1940" (NBER Working Paper no. 22910, March 2017), http://nber.org/papers /w22910.

7.   James Manyika et al., *The US Economy: An Agenda for Inclusive Growth*, McKinsey Global Institute, November 2016, 6.

8.   Edward Alden and Rebecca Strauss, *How America Stacks Up: Economic Competitiveness and U.S. Policy* (New York: Council on Foreign Relations, 2016).

9.   James Manyika et al., *Jobs Lost, Jobs Gained: Workforce Transitions in a Time of Automation*, McKinsey Global Institute, December 2017, http://mckinsey.com/mgi /overview/2017-in-review/automation-and-the-future-of-work/jobs-lost-jobs-gained -workforce-transitions-in-a-time-of-automation.

10. Christoph Lakner and Branko Milanovic, "Global Income Distribution: From the Fall of the Berlin Wall to the Great Recession" (The World Bank Policy Research Working Paper no. 6719, December 2013), http://documents.worldbank.org/curated /en/914431468162277879/pdf/WPS6719.pdf.

11. David H. Autor, David Dorn, and Gordon H. Hanson, "The China Shock: Learning From Labor Market Adjustment to Large Changes in Trade" (NBER Working Paper no. 21906, January 2016), http://nber.org/papers/w21906; Lawrence Edwards and Robert Z. Lawrence, *Rising Tide: Is Growth in Emerging Economies Good for the United States?* (Washington, DC: Peterson Institute for International Economics, 2013); Adams Nager, "Trade vs. Productivity: What Caused U.S. Manufacturing's Decline and How to Revive It," Information Technology & Innovation Foundation, February 2017, http:// www2.itif.org/2017-trade-vs-productivity.pdf.

12. Arun Sundarajan, "The Future of Work: The Digital Economy Will Sharply Erode the Traditional Employer-Employee Relationship," *Finance & Development* 54, no. 2 (June 2017).

13. Dick M. Carpenter II et al., *License to Work: A National Study of Burdens from Occupational Licensing* (Arlington, VA: Institute for Justice, 2017), http://ij.org /wp-content/themes/ijorg/images/ltw2/License_to_Work_2nd_Edition.pdf.

14. Mark Muro et al., *Digitalization and the American Workforce* (Washington, DC: Brookings Institution, 2017), http://brookings.edu/wp-content/uploads/2017/11 /mpp_2017nov15_digitalization_full_report.pdf.

15. Carl Benedikt Frey and Michael A. Osborne, "The Future of Employment: How Susceptible Are Jobs to Computerisation?," Oxford Martin Programme on Technology and Employment, September 2013, http://oxfordmartin.ox.ac.uk/downloads /academic/future-of-employment.pdf.

16. Manyika et al., *Jobs Lost, Jobs Gained*; James Manyika, "Technology, Jobs, and the Future of Work," McKinsey Global Institute, May 2017, http://mckinsey.com/global-themes /employment-and-growth/technology-jobs-and-the-future-of-work.

17. White House, "Artificial Intelligence, Automation, and the Economy," U.S. Council of Economic Advisers, December 2016, http://whitehouse.gov/sites/whitehouse.gov/files /images/EMBARGOED%20AI%20Economy%20Report.pdf.

18. Federal Reserve, "Record of Meeting: Community Advisory Council and Board of Governors," November 3, 2017, http://federalreserve.gov/aboutthefed/files/cac-20171103.pdf.

19. Spencer Overton, "The Impact of Automation on Black Jobs" (data compiled for *The Future of Work* CBCF ALC Issue Forum, September 23, 2017), http://jointcenter.org/sites/default/files/The%20Impact%20of%20Automation%20on%20Black%20Jobs%20CBC%20ALC%2011-14-17.pdf.

20. Michael Chui, James Manyika, and Mehdi Miremadi, "Four Fundamentals of Workplace Automation," *McKinsey Quarterly*, November 2015, http://mckinsey.com/business-functions/digital-mckinsey/our-insights/four-fundamentals-of-workplace-automation.

21. Bureau of Labor Statistics, "Web Developers," Occupational Outlook Handbook, http://bls.gov/ooh/computer-and-information-technology/web-developers.htm.

22. James Bessen, "How Computer Automation Affects Occupations: Technology, Jobs, and Skills," *Vox*, September 22, 2016, http://voxeu.org/article/how-computer-automation-affects-occupations.

23. Economists Laura Tyson and Michael Spence write: "Historical experience indicates that as technology has increased human productivity, the result has been net job creation, not net job destruction. In the past, with a lag and with painful adjustment costs for dislocated workers whose jobs have disappeared, technological progress has fostered growth in demand for new goods and services, and this has increased demand for labor and more than offset the labor-substituting effects of such progress." They also note that "the future outlook, however, is uncertain," and that job losses could be deeper and more lasting than in previous technological revolutions. "Exploring the Effects of Technology on Income and Wealth Inequality," in *After Piketty: The Agenda for Economics and Inequality*, ed. Heather Boushey, J. Bradford DeLong, and Marshall Steinbaum (Cambridge, MA: Harvard University Press, 2017).

24. *OECD Employment Outlook 2017* (Paris: OECD Publishing, 2017), http://www.oecd.org/els/oecd-employment-outlook-19991266.htm.

25. Burning Glass Technologies and Capitol One, "Crunched by the Numbers: The Digital Skills Gap in the Workforce," March 2015, http://burning-glass.com/wp-content/uploads/2015/06/Digital_Skills_Gap.pdf.

26. Sundarajan, "The Future of Work."

27. Manyika et al., *Jobs Lost, Jobs Gained*.

28. Klaus Schwab, *The Fourth Industrial Revolution* (New York: Crown Books, 2017).

29. John Maynard Keynes, "Economic Possibilities for Our Grandchildren," in *Essays in Persuasion* (New York: W. W. Norton, 1963), 358–373, http://www.econ.yale.edu/smith/econ116a/keynes1.pdf.

30. National Commission on Technology, Automation and Economic Progress, *Technology and the American Economy Volume 1*, Y3.T22-2T22 (Washington DC: GPO, 1966), http://files.eric.ed.gov/fulltext/ED023803.pdf.

31. Keith Bradsher and Paul Mozur, "China's Plan to Build Its Own High-Tech Industries Worries Western Businesses," *New York Times*, March 7, 2017, http://nytimes

.com/2017/03/07/business/china-trade-manufacturing-europe.html; Keith Bradsher, "China Hastens the World Toward an Electric-Car Future," *New York Times*, October 9, 2017, http://nytimes.com/2017/10/09/business/china-hastens-the-world-toward-an -electric-car-future.html.

32. Mike Henry, "US R&D Spending at All-Time High, Federal Share Reaches Record Low," American Institute of Physics, November 8, 2016, http://aip.org/fyi/2016 /us-rd-spending-all-time-high-federal-share-reaches-record-low.

33. Alden and Strauss, *How America Stacks Up*.

34. R&D Budget and Policy Program, "Historical Trends in Federal R&D," American Association for the Advancement of Science, http://aaas.org/page /historical-trends-federal-rd.

35. Donald J. Boyd, *Public Research Universities: Changes in State Funding* (Cambridge, MA: American Academy of Arts and Sciences, 2015), http://amacad.org/multimedia /pdfs/publications/researchpapersmonographs/PublicResearchUniv_ ChangesInStateFunding.pdf.

36. Charles W. Wessner and Alan Wolff, *Rising to the Challenge: U.S. Innovation Policy for the Global Economy* (Washington, DC: National Research Council, 2012); Office of the U.S. Trade Representative, "USTR Announces Section 301 Investigation of China," http://ustr.gov/about-us/policy-offices/press-office/press-releases/2017/august /ustr-announces-initiation-section.

37. The Commission on the Theft of American Intellectual Property, "The IP Commission Report," The National Bureau of Asian Research, 2013, http://ipcommission.org /report/ip_commission_report_052213.pdf.

38. Aaron Smith and Monica Anderson, "Automation in Everyday Life," Pew Research Center, October 4, 2017, http://pewinternet.org/2017/10/04 /automation-in-everyday-life.

39. "European Parliament Calls for Robot Law, Rejects Robot Tax," Reuters, February 16, 2017, http://reuters.com/article/us-europe-robots-lawmaking /european-parliament-calls-for-robot-law-rejects-robot-tax-idUSKBN15V2KM.

40. James Manyika et al., "Digital America: A Tale of the Haves and Have-Mores," McKinsey Global Institute, December 2015, http://mckinsey.com/industries/high-tech /our-insights/digital-america-a-tale-of-the-haves-and-have-mores.

41. Jeb Bush, Thomas F. McLarty, and Edward Alden, *U.S. Immigration Policy*, Independent Task Force Report no. 63 (New York: Council on Foreign Relations), 2009.

42. Stephanie Saul, "As Flow of Foreign Students Wanes, U.S. Universities Feel the Sting," *New York Times*, January 2, 2018, http://nytimes.com/2018/01/02/us/international -enrollment-drop.html; Stuart Anderson, "Here's What to Expect on Immigration in 2018," *Forbes*, January 2, 2018, http://forbes.com/sites/stuartanderson/2018/01/02 /heres-what-to-expect-on-immigration-in-2018/2.

43. "China Eases Visa Permits for Foreign High-Skilled Workers," *Xinhua*, January 4, 2018, http://xinhuanet.com/english/2018-01/04/c_136872071.htm.

44. Ian Hathaway and Robert E. Litan, *Declining Business Dynamism in the United States: A Look at States and Metros*, Brookings Institution, May 2014, http://brookings.edu

/research/declining-business-dynamism-in-the-united-states-a-look-at-states-and
-metros; Michael J. Coren, "The Number of New Business in the US Is Falling Off a
Cliff," *Quartz*, May 24, 2016, http://qz.com/690881/the-number-of-new-businesses
-in-the-us-is-falling-off-a-cliff.

45. Geoff Colvin, "The Surprising Slowdown in Startups," *Fortune*, May 18, 2016, http://
fortune.com/2016/03/18/startup-growth-stagnation.

46. Jim Tankersley, "A Very Bad Sign for All but America's Biggest Cities," *Washington Post*,
May 22, 2016, http://washingtonpost.com/news/wonk
/wp/2016/05/22/a-very-bad-sign-for-all-but-americas-biggest-cities.

47. Jay Shambaugh et al., *Thirteen Facts About Wage Growth*.

48. Jay Shambaugh and Ryan Nunn, "Why Wages Aren't Growing in America," *Harvard
Business Review*, October 24, 2017, http://hbr.org/2017/10/why-wages-arent
-growing-in-america.

49. Shambaugh et al., *Thirteen Facts About Wage Growth*.

50. *OECD Employment Outlook 2017*; International Labor Organization and the
Organization for Economic Cooperation and Development, "The Labour Share in G20
Economies," February 2015, http://oecd.org/g20/topics/employment-and-social
-policy/The-Labour-Share-in-G20-Economies.pdf.

51. Jared Bernstein, "What's the Matter With Wages? Exploring Wage Stagnation and the
American Worker" (presentation at the Brookings Institution, September 26, 2017),
http://hamiltonproject.org/events/whats_the_matter_with_wages_exploring_wage_
stagnation_and_the_american_work.

52. Bureau of Labor Statistics, "Alternative Measures of Labor Underutilization,"
Economic News Release, http://www.bls.gov/news.release/empsit.t15.htm. The
Federal Reserve recently noted that barriers to economic stability continue to
disproportionately affect people of color and disabled workers; unemployment among
African Americans was nearly 8 percent and among persons with a disability
10.5 percent in 2016.

53. Shambaugh et al., *Thirteen Facts About Wage Growth*; Steve Levine, "Good News:
Inequality Shrinking," *Axios*, December 6, 2017, http://axios.com/the-shrinking-of
-inequality-2515429929.html.

54. Larger forces may be at work as well: rising wage inequality and a growing share of the
gains accruing to capital rather than labor appear to be characteristic of the early stages
of eras of rapid technological change. Similar trends were evident in the early stages of
the Industrial Revolution. As MGI has argued, times of economic disruption and
transition can have painful consequences for many workers. In early Industrial
Revolution Britain, wage growth stagnated for roughly the first half of the nineteenth
century even as new investments in mechanical spinning, steam engines, and other
technologies raised productivity sharply and the rate of company profits doubled. It was
only after the middle part of the century—when capital investments reached a scale
large enough to have absorbed the available labor supplies—that wage growth began to
keep pace with, and eventually overtake, productivity growth. It remains to be seen
whether our modern technological revolution will follow the same trend. See Robert C.
Allen, "Engels' Pause: Technical Change, Capital Accumulation, and Inequality in the

British Industrial Revolution," *Explorations in Economic History* 46, no. 4 (October 2009).

55. Bureau of Labor Statistics, "Fastest Growing Occupations 2014-24," Economic News Release, http://www.bls.gov/news.release/ecopro.t05.htm.

56. Bureau of Labor Statistics, "Occupations With the Most Job Growth," Employment Projections, http://www.bls.gov/emp/ep_table_104.htm.

57. *OECD Employment Outlook 2017*, 29.

58. "Jobs for America's Graduates," http://jag.org; "Generation," http://generation.org.

59. Sarah Holder, "America's Most and Least Distressed Cities," CityLab, September 25, 2016, http://citylab.com/equity/2017/09/distressed-communities/541044.

60. Robert J. Gordon, *The Rise and Fall of American Growth* (Princeton, NJ: Princeton University Press, 2016).

61. Claudia Goldin, "America's Graduation From High School: The Evolution and Spread of Secondary Schooling in the Twentieth Century," *Journal of Economic History* 58, no. 2 (1998): 345–374.

62. There has been significant slippage compared with other countries over the last generation, however: Americans aged fifty-five to sixty-four still rank first worldwide in both high school and college completion; the generation aged twenty-five to thirty-four has fallen to twelfth in both rankings. The picture is especially troubling for young people from poorer households. Rebecca Strauss, "Schooling Ourselves in an Unequal America," *Opinionator* (blog), *New York Times*, June 26, 2013, http://opinionator.blogs.nytimes.com/author/rebecca-strauss.

63. Bureau of Labor Statistics, "Job Openings and Labor Turnover Summary," Economic News Release, http://www.bls.gov/news.release/jolts.nr0.htm.

64. See Rachael Stephens, "Mind the Gap: The State of Skills in the U.S.," Third Way, July 2017, http://thirdway.org/report/mind-the-gap-the-state-of-skills-in-the-us.

65. Joan Richardson et al., eds., "The PDK Poll of the Public's Attitudes Toward the Public Schools," *Kappan* magazine, September 2017, http://pdkpoll.org/results.

66. Tyson and Spence, "Exploring the Effects of Technology on Inequality."

67. Anthony P. Carnevale, Tanya I. Garcia, and Artem Gulish, "Career Pathways: Five Ways to Connect College and Careers," Georgetown University's Center on Education and the Workforce, 2017, http://cew.georgetown.edu/wp-content/uploads/LEE-final.pdf.

68. Teresa Kroeger and Elise Gould, "The Class of 2017," Economic Policy Institute, 2017, http://epi.org/publication/the-class-of-2017.

69. "First Destinations for the College Class of 2016," National Association of Colleges and Employers, 2017, http://naceweb.org/uploadedfiles/files/2017/publication/report/first-destinations-for-the-college-class-of-2016.pdf.

70. Burning Glass Technologies, "The Art of Employment: How Liberal Arts Graduates Can Improve Their Labor Market Prospects," 2013, http://burning-glass.com/wp-content/uploads/BGTReportLiberalArts.pdf.

71. Federal Reserve Bank of New York, "Center for Microeconomic Data: Student Debt,"

2017, http://newyorkfed.org/microeconomics/databank.html; Bipartisan Policy Center, "America's Student Debt Explosion: Understanding the Federal Government's Role," March 2017, http://bipartisanpolicy.org/wp-content/uploads/2017/03/BPC-Higher -Education-Americas-Student-Debt-Explosion.pdf.

72. Anthony P. Carnevale et al., *Good Jobs That Pay Without a BA* (Washington, DC: Georgetown University's Center on Education and the Workforce, 2017), http:// goodjobsdata.org/wp-content/uploads/Good-Jobs-wo-BA.pdf.

73. Harry J. Holzer and Sandy Baum, *Making College Work* (Washington, DC: Brookings Institution Press, 2017).

74. Matt Sigelman, chief executive of Burning Glass Technologies, interview, November 22, 2017.

75. "Bridge the Gap: Rebuilding America's Middle Skills," Accenture, Burning Glass Technologies, and Harvard Business School, November 2014, http://hbs.edu /competitiveness/Documents/bridge-the-gap.pdf.

76. IBM, "Growing Digital Jobs and Advantage for Workers," IBM White Paper, 2017.

77. Robert Chiappetta, director of government affairs, Toyota Motor North America, interview, November 9, 2017.

78. Stephanie Cronen, Meghan McQuiggan, and Emily Isenberg, "Adult Training and Education: Results From the National Household Education Survey's Program of 2016," National Center for Education Statistics and the U.S. Department of Education, September 2017, http://nces.ed.gov/pubs2017/2017103.pdf.

79. National Skills Coalition, "Skills for Good Jobs: An Agenda for the Next President," November 2016, http://workforcedqc.org/sites/default/files/images/NSC%20 Skills%20for%20Good%20Jobs%20Agenda.pdf.

80. Joseph B. Fuller and Matthew Sigelman, "Room to Grow: Identifying New Frontiers for Apprenticeships," Harvard Business School and Burning Glass Technologies, November 2017, http://hbs.edu/managing-the-future-of-work/Documents/room-to -grow.pdf.

81. White House Office of the Press Secretary, "Fact Sheet: Investing $90 Million Through ApprenticeshipUSA to Expand Proven Pathways into the Middle Class," April 2016, http://obamawhitehouse.archives.gov/the-press-office/2016/04/21/fact-sheet -investing-90-million-through-apprenticeshipusa-expand-proven; Ian Kullgren and Marianne Levine, "Trump Signs Executive Order on Apprenticeships," *Politico*, June 15, 2017, http://politico.com/story/2017/06/15/ trump-apprenticeship-executive-order-239590.

82. "Using Labor Market Data to Improve Student Success," Aspen Institute, September 2016, http://aspeninstitute.org/publications/using-labor-market-data-improve -student-success.

83. Jason A. Tyszko, "Reinventing Employer Signaling in a Rapidly Changing Talent Marketplace," U.S. Chamber of Commerce Foundation, September 27, 2017, http:// uschamberfoundation.org/blog/post/reinventing-employer-signaling-rapidly -changing-talent-marketplace.

84. Credential Engine, http://credentialengine.org.

85. Aneesh Chopra and Ethan Gurwitz, "Modernizing America's Workforce Data Architecture," Center for American Progress, August 15, 2017, http:// americanprogress.org/issues/economy/reports/2017/08/15/437303 /modernizing-americas-workforce-data-architecture.

86. The Obama administration tried to go a step further by enacting the so-called gainful employment regulations, which would have required vocational programs at for-profit higher education institutions as well as nondegree programs at community colleges to meet certain targets for the debt-to-income ratios of their graduates, or risk losing access to federal financial aid. The goal was to avoid saddling students with heavy debts to obtain certificates that did not lead to good jobs. The private colleges sued the Department of Education to block the rule, which has since been frozen by the Trump administration. See Katoe Reilly, "'We Will Keep Suing.' 17 States Slam Betsy DeVos for Blocking Rules on For-Profit Colleges," *Time*, October 18, 2017, http://time .com/4987630/state-lawsuit-betsy-devos-for-profit-college.

87. Aneesh Chopra, former U.S. chief technology officer, interview, October 31, 2017.

88. Susan Scrivener et al., "Doubling Graduation Rates: Three-Year Effects of CUNY's Accelerated Study in Associate Programs (ASAP) for Developmental Education Students," MDRC, 2015, http://mdrc.org/publication/doubling-graduation-rates; Thomas Bailey, Shanna Smith Jaggars, and Davis Jenkins, "What We Know About Guided Pathways," Community College Research Center, April 2015, http://ccrc .tc.columbia.edu/publications/what-we-know-about-guided-pathways-packet.html.

89. Byron Auguste, interview, November 15, 2017.

90. Journeys, http://informjourneys.com.

91. John Donovan and Cathy Benko, "AT&T's Talent Overhaul," *Harvard Business Review*, October 2016.

92. "What Employers Can Do to Encourage Their Workers to Retrain," *Economist*, January 14, 2017, http://www.economist.com/news/special-report/21714171-companies-are -embracing-learning-core-skill-what-employers-can-do-encourage-their.

93. Brad Stone, "Costco CEO Craig Jelinek Leads the Cheapest, Happiest Company in the World," *Bloomberg BusinessWeek*, June 7, 2013.

94. Michael Corkery, "At Walmart Academy, Training Better Managers. But With a Better Future?" *New York Times*, August 8, 2017, http://nytimes.com/2017/08/08/business /walmart-academy-employee-training.html.

95. "What You Need to Know About Amazon's New Career Choice Program," *TeachThought*, January 19, 2018, http://teachthought.com/current-events /what-you-need-to-know-about-amazons-new-career-choice-program.

96. Amanda Bergson-Shilcock, "NSC's New Report Explores Role of Skill-Building for Service-Sector Workers," *Skills* (blog), National Skills Coalition, February 15, 2017, http://nationalskillscoalition.org/news/blog/nscs-new-report-explores-role-of-skill -building-for-service-sector-workers.

97. Kimberly Gilsdorf and Fay Hanleybrown, *Investing in Entry-Level Talent* (Reimagining Social Change, 2017), http://fsg.org/publications/investing-entry-level -talent#download-area; Neil Irwin, "How Did Walmart Get Cleaner Stores and Higher

Sales? It Paid Its People More," *New York Times*, October 15, 2016, http://nytimes
.com/2016/10/16/upshot/how-did-walmart-get-cleaner-stores-and-higher-sales-it-paid
-its-people-more.html.

98. "SkillsFuture," Government of Singapore, Ministry of Manpower, October 25, 2016,
http://mom.gov.sg/employment-practices/skills-training-and-development/skillsfuture.

99. Rick McHugh and Will Kimball, "How Low Can We Go? State Unemployment
Insurance Programs Exclude Record Numbers of Jobless Workers," Economic Policy
Institute, Briefing Paper no. 392, March 9, 2015, http://epi.org/publication
/how-low-can-we-go-state-unemployment-insurance-programs-exclude-record
-numbers-of-jobless-workers.

100. Conor McKay, Ethan Pollack, and Alistair Fitzpayne, *Modernizing Unemployment
Insurance for the Changing Nature of Work* (Washington, DC: Aspen Institute Future of
Work Initiative, January 2018).

101. Alden and Strauss, *How America Stacks Up.*

102. "Labor Force Participation Rate," OECD, May 29, 2017, http://data.oecd.org/emp
/labour-force-participation-rate.htm.

103. Alden and Strauss, *How America Stacks Up.*

104. Ibid.

105. Amanda Bergson-Shilcock, "Congress Should Invest in Adult Basic Education,"
National Skills Coalition, March 3, 2016, http://nationalskillscoalition.org/resources
/publications/file/Why-Congress-should-invest-in-adult-basic-education.pdf.

106. When the TAA program was created by President John F. Kennedy in 1962, many
critics pointed out the illogic of providing special benefits for workers displaced by trade
as opposed to those displaced due to technology or resource exhaustion, changing
consumer preferences, or myriad other causes. But Kennedy argued that because trade
liberalization was policy deliberately pursued by government, it was rightly seen as
different. "When considerations of national policy make it desirable to avoid higher
tariffs, those injured by that competition should not be required to bear the full brunt of
the impacts," he said. Over time, TAA became part of the political bargain that
persuaded some Democrats to support trade agreements. See the discussion in Edward
Alden, *Failure to Adjust: How Americans Got Left Behind in the Global Economy* (Lanham,
MD: Rowman & Littlefield, 2017).

107. David H. Autor, David Dorn, and Gordon H. Hanson, "The China Syndrome: Local
Labor Market Effects of Import Competition in the United States" (NBER Working
Paper no. 18054, May 2012), http://nber.org/papers/w18054.

108. Wolters Kluwer Health: Lippincott Williams and Wilkins, "High Prevalence of Opioid
Use by Social Security Disability Recipients," *Science Daily*, August 14, 2014, http://
sciencedaily.com/releases/2014/08/140814123612.htm.

109. "Back to Work Sweden: Improving the Re-Employment Prospects of Displaced
Workers, Executive Summary," OECD, 2015, http://oecd.org/employment/emp
/Sweden-BTW-DocsPress-ENG.pdf.

110. Alden and Strauss, *How America Stacks Up.*

111. *OECD Employment Outlook 2017*.

112. Heather Long, "There Are 7 Million Unemployed and 6.2 Million Job Openings. What's the Problem?" *Washington Post*, August 8, 2017, http://washingtonpost.com /news/wonk/wp/2017/08/08/there-are-7-million-unemployed-and-6-2-million -job-openings-whats-the-problem.

113. David Ihrke, "United States Mover Rate at a New Record Low," *Census* (blog), January 23, 2017, http:// www. census.gov/newsroom/blogs/random-samplings/2017/01 /mover-rate.html.

114. Ashley Pettus, "Immobile Labor," *Harvard* magazine, January–February 2013, http:// harvardmagazine.com/2013/01/immobile-labor.

115. Jeffrey Lin, "Technological Adaptation, Cities, and the New Work" (Federal Reserve Bank of Philadelphia Working Paper no. 09-17, July 2009), http://philadelphiafed.org /-/media/research-and-data/publications/working-papers/2009/wp09-17.pdf.

116. Rebecca Diamond, "The Determinants and Welfare Implications of US Workers' Diverging Location Choices by Skill: 1980–2000," *American Economic Review* 106, no. 3 (March 2016): 479–524, http://aeaweb.org/articles?id=10.1257/aer.20131706.

117. Compare with Jon Kamp, "Far From Boston, Faded Industrial Hubs Grasp for Growth," *Wall Street Journal*, August 8, 2017, http://wsj.com/articles/far-from-boston-faded -industrial-hub-grasps-for-growth-1502213302; see also Janet Adamy and Paul Overberg, "Struggling Americans Once Sought Greener Pastures—Now They're Stuck," *Wall Street Journal*, August 2, 2017, http://wsj.com/articles /struggling-americans-once-sought-greener-pasturesnow-theyre-stuck-1501686801.

118. Gillian B. White, "How Zoning Laws Exacerbate Inequality," *Atlantic*, November 23, 2015, http://theatlantic.com/business/archive/2015/11/zoning-laws-and-the-rise-of -economic-inequality/417360; Peter Ganong and Daniel W. Shoag, "Why Has Regional Income Convergence in the U.S. Declined?" (NBER Working Paper no. 23609, November 2017), http://nber.org/papers/w23609.

119. Chang Tai-Hsieh and Enrico Moretti, "Housing Constraints and Spatial Misallocation" (NBER Working Paper no. 21154, May 2017), http://nber.org/papers/w21154.pdf.

120. Robert Collinson, Ingrid Gould Ellen, and Jens Ludwig, "Low-Income Housing Policy" (NBER Working Paper no. 21071, April 2015), http://nber.org/papers/w21071.pdf. The federal government spends about $40 billion a year on various forms of support for low-income housing, primarily for renters; in comparison, the mortgage-interest deduction, which disproportionately benefits wealthier homeowners, costs the Treasury Department about $190 billion annually.

121. Elizabeth Kneebone and Natalie Holmes, "The Growing Distance Between People and Jobs in Metropolitan America," Brookings Institution, March 2015, http://brookings .edu/research/the-growing-distance-between-people-and-jobs-in -metropolitan-america.

122. Matt Barnum, "The Certification Maze: Why Teachers Who Cross State Lines Can't Find Their Way Back to the Classroom," *74*, February 15, 2017, http://the74million .org/article/the-certification-maze-why-teachers-who-cross-state-lines-cant-find-their -way-back-to-the-classroom.

123. Dan Goldhaber et al., "Barriers to Cross-State Mobility in the Teaching Profession: Evidence From Oregon and Washington," Calder National Center for Analysis of Longitudinal Data in Education Research, October 2015, http://caldercenter.org/sites /default/files/WP%20143%20Policy%20Brief.pdf.

124. Janna E. Johnson and Morris M. Kleiner, "Is Occupational Licensing a Barrier to Interstate Migration?," Federal Reserve Bank of Minnesota, December 2017, http:// minneapolisfed.org/research/sr/sr561.pdf.

125. Morris M. Kleiner, "Reforming Occupational Licensing Policies," Brookings Institution, 2015, http://brookings.edu/wp-content/uploads/2016/06/THP_ KleinerDiscPaper_final.pdf.

126. Jaison R. Abel, Richard Deitz, and Yaqin Su, "Are Recent College Graduates Finding Good Jobs?" *Current Issues in Economics and Finance* 20, no. 1 (January 2014), http:// newyorkfed.org/medialibrary/media/research/current_issues/ci20-1.pdf.

127. Joseph B. Fuller and Manjari Raman, "Dismissed by Degrees: How Degree Inflation Is Undermining U.S. Competitiveness and Hurting America's Middle Class," Accenture, Grads of Life, Harvard Business School, 2017, http://www.hbs.edu/managing-the -future-of-work/Documents/dismissed-by-degrees.pdf.

128. Burning Glass Technologies, "How Demand for a Bachelor's Degree Is Reshaping the Workforce," September 2014, http://burning-glass.com/wp-content/uploads/Moving_ the_Goalposts.pdf.

129. Fuller and Raman, *Dismissed by Degrees.*

130. Manyika, "Technology, Jobs and the Future of Work."

131. Skills of Chicagoland's Future, "2016 Impact Report," May 2017, http:// skillsforchicagolandsfuture.com/wp-content/uploads/2017/05/2016-Annual-Report_ Final_web.pdf; see also Skills for Rhode Island's Future, http://skillsforri.com.

132. "Evaluation of a Demand Driven Workforce Solution," Skills for Chicagoland's Future Evaluation Project 2017, August 2017, http://skillsforchicagolandsfuture.com /wp-content/uploads/2017/10/2017-SCF-New-Growth-Report.pdf.

133. White House, "TechHire Initiative," 2015, http://obamawhitehouse.archives.gov /node/325231.

134. Lawrence F. Katz and Alan B. Krueger, "The Rise and Nature of Alternative Work Arrangements in the United States, 1995-2015" (NBER Working Paper no. 22667, September 2016), http://nber.org/papers/w22667.

135. Lael Brainard, "The Gig Economy: Implications of the Growth of Contingent Work" (speech at the Evolution of Work conference, New York, November 17, 2016), http:// bis.org/review/r161128d.htm.

136. Noam Scheiber, "Tax Law Offers a Carrot to Gig Workers. But It May Have Costs," *New York Times*, December 31, 2017, http://nytimes.com/2017/12/31/business /economy/tax-work.html; Shuyi Oei and Diane M. Ring, "The Senate Tax Bill and the Battles over Worker Classification," *TaxProf* (blog), November 11, 2017, http://taxprof .typepad.com/taxprof_blog/2017/11/the-senate-tax-bill-and-worker-classification .html; Valerie Bolden-Barrett, "The Burgeoning Gig Economy Gets a Boost—From the New Tax Bill," *HRDive*, January 8, 2018, http://hrdive.com/news/the-burgeoning

-gig-economy-gets-a-boost-from-the-new-tax-bill/514227.

137. Employer-provided health insurance in the United States was something of a historical accident. During World War II, the War Labor Board, responsible for overseeing wartime wage and price controls, ruled that fringe benefits such as health insurance and sick leave did not qualify as "wages" and thus were exempt from the restrictions. Employers facing labor shortage responded by offering more generous benefits packages. After the war, employer-sponsored coverage became the norm, with the number of Americans covered by employer health plans growing sevenfold by 1960.

138. Bureau of Labor Statistics, "Retirement Benefits: Access, Participation, and Take-up Rates," Employee Benefits Survey, March 2016, http://www.bls.gov/ncs/ebs/benefits/2016/ownership/private/table02a.htm.

139. Bureau of Labor Statistics, "Table 6. Selected Paid Leave Benefits: Access," National Compensation Survey, March 2017, http://www.bls.gov/news.release/ebs2.t06.htm.

140. "OECD Indicators of Employment Protection," July 2013, OECD, http://oecd.org/employment/emp/oecdindicatorsofemploymentprotection.htm.

141. Board of Governors of the Federal Reserve System, *Report on the Economic Well-Being of U.S. Households in 2016* (Washington, DC: Federal Reserve Board, 2017), http://federalreserve.gov/publications/files/2016-report-economic-well-being-us-households-201705.pdf.

142. Diana Farrell and Fiona Greig, "The Monthly Stress-Test on Family Finances," JPMorgan Chase Institute Insight, March 2017, http://jpmorganchase.com/corporate/institute/insight-financial-stress-test.htm.

143. Sophie Quinton, "With the Growth of the Gig Economy, States Rethink How Workers Get Benefits," *Stateline* (blog), Pew Charitable Trusts, February 22, 2017, http://pewtrusts.org/en/research-and-analysis/blogs/stateline/2017/02/22/with-growth-of-the-gig-economy-states-rethink-how-workers-get-benefits.

144. Nick Reisman, "Cuomo Plans Task Force to Assess 'Gig Economy' Benefits," *State of Politics* (blog), January 11, 2017, http://nystateofpolitics.com/2017/01/cuomo-plans-task-force-to-assess-gig-economy-impact.

145. *OECD Employment Outlook 2017*, 84.

146. Gordon, *The Rise and Fall of American Growth*, 563.

147. Louis Nelson, "Trump at Davos: 'America Is Open for Business,'" *Politico*, January 26, 2018, http://politico.com/story/2018/01/26/trump-davos-speech-2018-370860.

148. The tax bill is estimated by the Congressional Budget Office to add nearly $1.5 trillion to the federal budget deficit over the next decade. For background on the debt and deficit problem and the coming challenges for the United States, see Alden and Strauss, *How America Stacks Up*.

149. Economics & Statistics Administration, "Foreign Direct Investment in the United States: Update to 2013 Report," U.S. Department of Commerce, http://esa.gov/reports/foreign-direct-investment-united-states-update-2013-report.

150. Matthew Rees and Matthew Slaughter, "Slaughter & Rees Report: The Global Economy and Domestic Jobs," Tuck School of Business, http://tuck.dartmouth.edu

/news/articles/research-contradicts-notion-that-exporting-jobs-hurts
-american-workers.

151. For Obama's investment statement, see White House Office of the Press Secretary, "Statement by the President on United States Commitment to Open Investment Policy," June 20, 2011, http://obamawhitehouse.archives.gov/the-press-office/2011/06/20 /statement-president-united-states-commitment-open-investment-policy.

152. Mihir Desai, "Breaking Down the New U.S. Corporate Tax Law," interview by Sarah Green Carmichael, December 26, 2017, *Harvard Business Review*, http://hbr.org /ideacast/2017/12/breaking-down-the-new-u-s-corporate-tax-law.

153. The administration's fiscal year 2019 budget proposes $200 billion in new federal spending, half to be awarded through competitive grants. See Office of Management and Budget (OMB), "Efficient, Effective, Accountable: An American Budget," http:// whitehouse.gov/wp-content/uploads/2018/02/budget-fy2019.pdf. The proposal has faced criticisms from some state and local officials who say it will offload more of the infrastructure burden on governments with fewer revenue sources. See Patrick Sisson, "Trump's Infrastructure Plan: Small Federal Investment, More State and Local Control," *Curbed*, February 12, 2018, http://curbed.com/2018/2/12/17003730 /trump-infrastructure-plan-funding-road-congress.

154. John Wagner, "U.S. Chamber of Commerce to Push Trump, Congress to Raise the Gas Tax to Fund Infrastructure," *Washington Post*, January 16, 2018.

155. OECD, *Action Plan on Base Erosion and Profit Shifting* (Paris: OECD Publishing, 2013), http://oecd.org/ctp/BEPSActionPlan.pdf.

156. Jennifer Harris, "Writing New Rules for the U.S.-China Investment Relationship," Council on Foreign Relations, December 2017, http://cfr.org/report/writing-new-rules -us-china-investment-relationship.

157. National Governors Association (NGA) Center for Best Practices, "Top Trends in State Economic Development," NGA, August 19, 2013, http://nga.org/files/live/sites/NGA /files/pdf/2013/1308TopTrendsinStateEconDevPaper.pdf; NGA Center for Best Practices, "Revisiting Top Trends in State Economic Development," NGA, March 2, 2016, http://nga.org/files/live/sites/NGA/files/pdf/2016/1603RevisitingTopTrends StateEcoDevelopment.pdf.

158. On Prosperity NOLA, see "About the New Orleans Business Alliance," New Orleans Business Alliance, http://nolaba.org/about; on Advance KC, see "Advance KC: A Strategic Blueprint for the City's Future," Advance KC, City of Kansas City, Missouri, http://kcmo.gov/advancekc; on Metro Phoenix, see "Metro Phoenix Global Investment Plan: The Global Cities Initiative, A Joint Project of Brookings and JPMorgan Chase," Greater Phoenix Economic Council, http://gpec.org/wp-content /uploads/2016/09/FDI-Plan-2017_Plan-2.pdf.

159. Henry M. Cothran, Derek Farnsworth, and Jennifer L. Clark, "Business Retention and Expansion Programs: Why Existing Businesses Are Important," University of Florida IFAS Extension, 2006, http://edis.ifas.ufl.edu/pdffiles/FE/FE65100.pdf.

160. One example of this sort of planning is the Global Cities Initiative, a joint project of the Brookings Institution and JPMorgan Chase that is helping civic leaders in U.S. cities

reorient their economies for better competitive success in global markets. See http://brookings.edu/project/global-cities.

161. Rodrick Miller, "The Tortoise and the Hare: Economic Competitiveness in the Amazon Era," *FDI Alliance*, December 2017, http://docs.wixstatic.com/ugd/a90217_bef9f493000c452f95da4f4db96376c2.pdf.

162. Nathan M. Jensen, "The Effect of Economic Development Incentives and Clawback Provisions on Job Creation: A Pre-registered Evaluation of Maryland and Virginia Programs," *Research & Politics* 4, no. 2 (June 2017), http://journals.sagepub.com/doi/full/10.1177/2053168017713646.

163. Good Jobs First, "Model Legislation for Subsidy Reforms," October 10, 2012, http://goodjobsfirst.org/accountable-development/model-legislation.

164. Karen Mills and Chris Rudnicki, "How Companies Can Help Rebuild America's Common Resources," *Harvard Business Review*, September 21, 2015, http://hbr.org/2015/09/how-companies-can-help-rebuild-americas-common-resources.

165. "America's Community Banks Hope for Lighter Regulation," *Economist*, June 1, 2017, http://economist.com/news/finance-and-economics/21722893-other-challenges-include-technology-staff-retention-succession-planning-and-thin.

166. Community Advisory Council and the Board of Governors, "Record of Meeting," November 2017, http://federalreserve.gov/aboutthefed/files/cac-20171103.pdf.

167. Johns Hopkins 21st Century Cities Initiative, "Financing Baltimore's Growth: Measuring Small Companies' Access to Capital," September 2017, http://21cc.jhu.edu/wp-content/uploads/2017/09/21cc-financing-baltimores-growth-sept-2017.pdf.

168. Dane Stangler and Jason Wiens, "The Economic Case for Welcoming Immigrant Entrepreneurs," Ewing Marion Kauffman Foundation, September 8, 2015, http://kauffman.org/what-we-do/resources/entrepreneurship-policy-digest/the-economic-case-for-welcoming-immigrant-entrepreneurs; Alexandra Starr, "Latino Immigrant Entrepreneurs: How to Capitalize on Their Economic Potential," Council on Foreign Relations, September 2012, http://cfr.org/report/latino-immigrant-entrepreneurs; Jason Wiens and Chris Jackson, "The Importance of Young Firms for Economic Growth," New American Economy, September 13, 2015, http://newamericaneconomy.org/issues/entrepreneurship.

169. Mark Warner, "Sens. Warner, Moran Reintroduce the Bipartisan Start Up Act," Press Release, September 29, 2017, http://warner.senate.gov/public/index.cfm/pressreleases?id=3F42A369-961C-4B4F-B6F4-DEA5BA28CCD8.

170. Dane Stangler and Jared Konczal, "Give Me Your Entrepreneurs, Your Innovators: Estimating the Impact of a Startup Visa," Ewing Marion Kauffman Foundation, February, 2013, http://kauffman.org/what-we-do/research/2013/02/give-me-your-entrepreneurs-your-innovators-estimating-employment-impact-of-a-startup-visa.

171. R&D Budget and Policy Program, "Historical Trends in Federal R&D," American Association for the Advancement of Science, September 2017, http://aaas.org/page/historical-trends-federal-rd#Overview; National Research Council, *Rising to the Challenge: U.S. Innovation Policy for the Global Economy* (Washington, DC: National Academies Press, 2012).

172. John F. Sargent Jr., "Federal Research and Development Funding FY2018," *Congressional Research Service*, August 14, 2017, http://fas.org/sgp/crs/misc/R44888 .pdf; Chris Mooney and Steven Mufson, "White House Seeks 72 Percent Cut to Clean Energy Research, Underscoring Administration's Preference for Fossil Fuels," *Washington Post*, February 1, 2018, http://washingtonpost.com/business/economy /white-house-seeks-72-percent-cut-to-clean-energy-research-underscoring -administrations-preference-for-fossil-fuelsv/2018/01/31/c2c69350-05f3-11e8-b48c -b07fea957bd5_story.html; Giorgia Guglielmi et al., "Trump Budget Gives Last-Minute Reprieve to Science Funding," *Nature*, February 12, 2018, http://nature.com/articles /d41586-018-01811-x.

173. "China May Match or Beat America in AI," *Economist*, July 15, 2017, http://economist .com/news/business/21725018-its-deep-pool-data-may-let-it-lead -artificial-intelligence-china-may-match-or-beat-america.

174. See Matt Hourihan, "If Government Scales Back Technology Research, Should We Expect Industry to Step In?" American Association for the Advancement of Science, October 16, 2017, http://mcmprodaaas.s3.amazonaws.com/s3fs-public/AAAS%20 Public%20%26%20Private%20R%26D.pdf.

175. Joe Kennedy and Robert D. Atkinson, "Why Expanding the R&D Tax Credit Is Key to Successful Corporate Tax Reform," Information Technology & Innovation Foundation, July 5, 2017, http://itif.org/publications/2017/07/05/why-expanding-rd-tax-credit-key -successful-corporate-tax-reform.

176. U.S. Department of Commerce, *Manufacturing USA Annual Report*, 2016, http:// manufacturingusa.com/sites/prod/files/Manufacturing%20USA-Annual%20 Report-FY%202016-web.pdf.

177. National Academies of Sciences, Engineering, and Medicine, *Securing Advanced Manufacturing in the United States* (Washington, DC: The National Academies Press, 2017), http://doi.org/10.17226/24875.

178. National Research Council Committee for Capitalizing on Science, Technology, and Innovation, *An Assessment of the Small Business Innovation Research Program* (Washington, DC: National Academies Press, 2008), http://ncbi.nlm.nih.gov/books /NBK23747.

179. Alden and Strauss, *How America Stacks Up*, 185.

180. National Academies of Sciences, Engineering, and Medicine, *Immigration Policy and the Search for Skilled Workers: Summary of a Workshop* (Washington, DC: National Academies Press, 2015), http://doi.org/10.17226/20145.

181. The Stopping Trained in America PhDs from Leaving the Economy (STAPLE) Act, first introduced by then Representative Jeff Flake (R-AZ) in 2009, would provide a fast track to permanent residence for foreign students earning PhDs in the STEM fields at American universities. It has been reintroduced in subsequent Congresses.

182. The Trump administration has taken several steps to raise hurdles for U.S. companies trying to bring in foreign, college-educated workers on the H-1B visa, which allows eighty-five thousand foreign workers to enter the United States each year on renewable three-year visas. See Stuart Anderson, "Here's What to Expect on Immigration in 2018," *Forbes*, January 2, 2018, http://forbes.com/sites/stuartanderson/2018/01/02

/heres-what-to-expect-on-immigration-in-2018. A broader set of recommendations for attracting and retaining highly skilled immigrants can be found in Bush, McLarty, and Alden, *U.S. Immigration Policy*.

183. Grant Gross, "Microsoft Calls for $5 Billion Investment in U.S. Education," *Computerworld*, September 27, 2012, http://computerworld.com/article/2491741 /technology-law-regulation/microsoft-calls-for--5b-investment-in-u-s--education.html.

184. Stephen Ezell, "ITIF Filing to USTR on Section 301 Investigation of China's Policies and Practices Related to Tech Transfer, IP, and Innovation," Information Technology & Innovation Foundation, October 25, 2017, http://itif.org/publications/2017/10/25 /itif-filing-ustr-section-301-investigation-chinas-policies-and-practices.

185. Julie Wagner et al., "12 Principles Guiding Innovation Districts," *Metropolitan Revolution Brookings*, September 8, 2017, http://brookings.edu/blog /metropolitan-revolution/2017/09/08/12-principles-guiding-innovation-districts-2.

186. "Global Cities Initiative: A Joint Project of Brookings and JPMorgan Chase," Brookings Institution, August 18, 2017, http://brookings.edu/project/global-cities.

187. Michael Porter and Jan Rivkin, "Choosing the United States," *Harvard Business Review*, March 2012, http://hbr.org/2012/03/choosing-the-united-states.

188. Steve Holt, *Periodic Payment of the Earned Income Tax Credit Revisited* (Washington, DC: Brookings Institution, 2015), http://brookings.edu/research/periodic-payment-of-the -earned-income-tax-credit-revisited.

189. See Michael R. Strain, *Getting Back to Work* (Washington, DC: Conservative Reform Network, 2016), http://conservativereform.com/wp-content/uploads/2016/07/CRN_ Employment_FINAL.pdf; Gene B. Sperling, "A Tax Proposal That Could Lift Millions Out of Poverty," *Atlantic*, October 17, 2017, http://theatlantic.com/business /archive/2017/10/eitc-for-all/542898.

190. Stanley Chrystal, "Beyond the Draft: Rethinking National Service," Aspen Institute, November 30, 2015, http://aspeninstitute.org/blog-posts/general-stanley-mcchrystal -beyond-draft-rethinking-national-service.

191. Clive Belfield, *The Economic Value of National Service* (Washington, DC: The Franklin Project, Aspen Institute, 2013), http://assets.aspeninstitute.org/content/uploads/files /content/docs/pubs/FranklinProject_EconomicValue_final.pdf.

192. Alan Manning, "The Truth About the Minimum Wage," *Foreign Affairs* 97, no. 1 (January/February 2018).

193. Ekaterina Jardim, et al., "Minimum Wage Increases, Wages, and Low-Wage Employment: Evidence From Seattle" (NBER Working Paper no. 23532, National Bureau of Economic Research, June 2017), http://nber.org/papers/w23532; Rachel West, "Five Flaws in a New Analysis of Seattle's Minimum Wage," Center for American Progress, June 28, 2017, http://www.americanprogress.org/issues/poverty /news/2017/06/28/435220/five-flaws-new-analysis-seattles-minimum-wage; and "University of Washington Analysis of Seattle Minimum Wage Increase Is Fundamentally Flawed," Press Release, Economic Policy Institute, June 26, 2017, http:// epi.org/press/university-of-washington-analysis-of-seattle-minimum-wage-increase -is-fundamentally-flawed.

194. Cynthia Miller et al., *Expanding the Earned Income Tax Credit for Workers Without Dependent Children* (New York: MDRC, 2017), http://mdrc.org/publication /expanding-earned-income-tax-credit-workers-without-dependent-children.

195. "Rethinking the EITC," Center for Economic Progress, October 14, 2015, http:// economicprogress.org/content/rethinking-eitc.

196. Bob Keener, "New Report: High-Road Business Practices Benefit Businesses and Society; Need Public Policy to Spread Adoption," American Sustainable Business Council, October 24, 2017, http://asbcouncil.org/news/press-release/new-report-high -road-business-practices-benefit-businesses-and-society; Zaynep Ton, *The Good Jobs Strategy: How the Smartest Companies Invest in Employees to Lower Costs and Boost Profits* (New York: New Harvest, 2014).

197. Larry Fink, "A Sense of Purpose: Larry Fink's Annual Letter to CEOs," BlackRock, January 2018, http://blackrock.com/corporate/en-no/investor-relations /larry-fink-ceo-letter.

198. Benefit Corporation, http://benefitcorp.net; James Surowiecki, "Companies With Benefits," *New Yorker*, August 4, 2014, http://newyorker.com/magazine/2014/08/04 /companies-benefits.

199. "The 2017 Distressed Communities Index," Economic Innovation Group, 2017, http:// eig.org/dci.

200. "Globalisation Has Marginalised Many Regions in the Rich World," *Economist*, October 21, 2017, http://economist.com/news/briefing/21730406-what-can-be-done -help-them-globalisation-has-marginalised-many-regions-rich-world.

201. A. E. Challinor, "Canada's Immigration Policy: A Focus on Human Capital," Migration Policy Institute, September 15, 2011, http://migrationpolicy.org/article/canadas -immigration-policy-focus-human-capital.

202. "2016 Broadband Progress Report," Federal Communication Commission, January 29, 2016, http://fcc.gov/reports-research/reports/broadband-progress-reports/2016 -broadband-progress-report.

203. Marguerite Reardon, "How Blazing Internet Speeds Helped Chattanooga Shed Its Smokestack Past," *CNET*, August 20, 2015, http://cnet.com/news/how-blazing -internet-speeds-helped-chattanooga-shed-its-smokestack-past; Dominic Rushe, "Chattanooga's Gig: How One City's Super-Fast Internet Is Driving a Tech Boom," *Guardian*, August 30, 2014, http://theguardian.com/world/2014/aug/30 /chattanooga-gig-high-speed-internet-tech-boom.

204. Matias Busso and Patrick Kline, "Do Local Economic Development Programs Work? Evidence From the Federal Empowerment Zone Program," University of Michigan's National Poverty Center, November 28, 2007, http://eml.berkeley.edu//~pkline/papers /Busso-Kline%20EZ%20(web).pdf.

205. Bruce Bartlett, "Enterprise Zones: A Bipartisan Failure," *Fiscal Times*, January 10, 2014, http://thefiscaltimes.com/Columns/2014/01/10/Enterprise-Zones-Bipartisan-Failure; U.S. Government Accountability Office, "Revitalization Programs: Empowerment Zones, Enterprise Communities, and Renewal Communities," March 12, 2010, http:// gao.gov/products/GAO-10-464R; Denis Teti, "An Idea Whose Time Never Came,"

Weekly Standard, January 15, 2016, http://weeklystandard.com/an-idea-whose-time
-never-came/article/2000593.

206. "Opportunity Zones," Economic Innovation Group, February 4, 2017,
http://eig.org/opportunityzones.

207. Concerns have been expressed, as with other programs that funnel capital into
distressed areas such as the EB-5 investor program, that this provision could open tax
loopholes subject to abuse. See, for example, Megan Schrader, "'Opportunity Zones' in
Tax Bill Ripe for Abuse," *Denver Post*, December 19, 2017, http://denverpost
.com/2017/12/19/opportunity-zones-in-gop-tax-bill-ripe-for-abuse.

208. Manish Pandey and James Townsend, "Provincial Nominee Programs: An Evaluation of
the Earnings and Retention Rates of Nominees" (Prairie Metropolis Centre Working
Paper Series WP11-04, July 25, 2011); Colin McCann, *Immigrant Entry to Smaller
Urban Centres and Coordination with Local Labour Markets in Canada: Effects of the
Provincial Nominee Program (PNP)* (Ottawa: University of Ottawa, December 2014),
http://ruor.uottawa.ca/handle/10393/32043.

209. Brandon Fuller and Sean Rust, "State-Based Visas: A Federalist Approach to Reforming
U.S. Immigration Policy," CATO Institute, April 23, 2014, http://cato.org/publications
/policy-analysis/state-based-visas-federalist-approach-reforming
-us-immigration-policy.

210. Antoine van Agtmael and Alfred Bakker, *The Smartest Places on Earth: Why the Rustbelts
Are the Emerging Hotspots of Global Innovation* (New York: Public Affairs, 2016).

211. "National Network: Connecting Learning and Work," http://nationalnetwork.org
/about.

212. See Vivian Hunt et al., "Delivering Through Diversity," McKinsey Global Institute,
January 2018, http://mckinsey.com/business-functions/organization/our-insights
/delivering-through-diversity.

213. See Swiss-American Chamber of Commerce, "Jobs Now: Swiss-Style Vocational
Education and Training: Voices for Companies, Governors and CEOs,"
http://www.ioe-emp.org/policy-areas/skills-and-education/skills-education-training
-news-details/article/gan-releases-jobs-now-report-on-vocational-training-swiss-style.

214. Terri Bergman and Deborah Kobes, *The State of Apprenticeship Among Workforce
Boards* (Washington, DC: National Association of Workforce Boards, 2017),
http://jff.org/publications/state-apprenticeship-among-workforce-boards.

215. "Careers and Apprenticeships," AFL-CIO, March 31, 2017, http://aflcio.org/about
/careers-and-apprenticeships.

216. Robert Schwartz and Nancy Hoffman, "Pathways to Upward Mobility," *National
Affairs*, Summer 2015, http://nationalaffairs.com/publications/detail
/pathways-to-upward-mobility.

217. "Credential Registry," Credential Engine, March 20, 2017, http://credentialengine.org.

218. Brent Parton, *Youth Apprenticeship in America Today* (Washington, DC: New America
Foundation, December 2017).

219. "CareerWise Connects Education and Industry to Benefit Students and Businesses,"
CareerWise Colorado, September 2016, http://careerwisecolorado.org/about

-overview; "CareerWise Colorado Gets an A," *Denver Post*, September 19, 2016, http://denverpost.com/2016/09/19/careerwise-colorado-gets-an-a.

220. Pathways to Prosperity Initiative, http://jff.org/initiatives/pathways-prosperity -network. The program has also produced an initial detailed case study looking at the rollout in Delaware. See Robert Rothman, "Propelling College and Career Success: The Role of Strategic Partnerships in Scaling Delaware Pathways," Pathways to Prosperity, 2017. The initiative was modeled after research by the Harvard Graduate School of Education; William C. Symonds, Robert Schwartz, and Ronald F. Ferguson, "Pathways to Prosperity: Meeting the Challenge of Preparing Young Americans for the 21st Century," Pathways to Prosperity Project, Harvard University Graduate School of Education, 2011, http://dash.harvard.edu/handle/1/4740480. Further details on the initiative to date are in Nancy Hoffman and Robert B. Schwartz, *Learning for Careers: The Pathways to Prosperity Network* (Cambridge, MA: Harvard Education Press, 2017).

221. Angela Hanks and Ethan Gurwitz, "How States Are Expanding Apprenticeship," Center for American Progress, February 9, 2016, http://americanprogress.org/issues /economy/reports/2016/02/09/130750/how-states-are-expanding-apprenticeship; NGA, "State Strategies to Scale Quality Work-Based Learning," October 31, 2016, http://nga.org/cms/home/nga-center-for-best-practices/center-publications/page-ehsw -publications/col2-content/main-content-list/state-strategies-to-scale-qualit.html.

222. "Colorado Governor John Hickenlooper, the Markle Foundation, and 20 States Launch the Skillful State Network; Introduce Skillful State Playbook," *Business Wire*, February 14, 2018, http://businesswire.com/news/home/20180214005998/en /Colorado-Governor-John-Hickenlooper-Markle-Foundation-20.

223. "Activate Incentive Funds for Work-Based Learning at Your School," Colorado Succeeds, January 31, 2018, http://coloradosucceeds.org/what-we-do/lead-initiatives /workforce-readiness/incentives-industry-credentials.

224. "Manufacturing Day Infographic," MFG Day, October 12, 2017, http://mfgday.com.

225. Holzer and Baum, *Making College Work*.

226. Organizations advocating universal computer science education in K-12 include the CSforAll Consortium (http://csforall.org/about) and Code.org (http://code.org).

227. Alastair Fitzpayne and Ethan Pollack, "A Changing Economy Requires a Renewed Focus on Lifelong Learning," Aspen Institute, July 5, 2017, http://aspeninstitute.org /blog-posts/a-changing-economy-requires-a-renewed-focus-on-lifelong-learning; Auta Main, *Maine's Lifelong Learning Accounts Good News for Workers, Businesses, and the Economy* (Boston: Federal Reserve Bank of Boston, 2008), http://maine.gov/labor /careerctr/docs/0908_lila_article.pdf; "Where Can Lifelong Learning Lead You?," Lifelong Learning Accounts, April 8, 2009, http://wtb.wa.gov /LifelongLearningAccount.asp.

228. Michael Mitchell et al., "A Lost Decade in Higher Education Funding: State Cuts Have Driven Up Tuition and Reduced Quality," Center on Budget and Policy Priorities, August 23, 2017, http://cbpp.org/research/state-budget-and-tax/a-lost-decade -in-higher-education-funding.

229. See Holzer and Baum, *Making College Work*.

230. Fitzpayne and Pollack, "A Changing Economy."

231. Edward Alden and Robert E. Litan, "A New Deal for the Twenty-First Century," Council on Foreign Relations, May 2017, http://cfr.org/report/new-deal-twenty-first-century.

232. James T. Austin et al., "Portable, Stackable Credentials: A New Education Model for Industry-Specific Career Pathways," McGraw-Hill Research Foundation, 2012, http://jff.org/publications/portable-stackable-credentials-new-education-model-industry-specific-career-pathways.

233. Tim Kaine, "Kaine, Portman Introduce Bipartisan Jobs Act to Help Workers Access Training for In-Demand Career Fields," January 25, 2017, http://kaine.senate.gov/press-releases/kaine-portman-introduce-bipartisan-jobs-act-to-help-workers-access-training-for-in-demand-career-fields.

234. In addition to greater funding, the Trump administration says it is pursuing ways to expand apprenticeships in sectors where they remain rare, such as health care, information technology, and advanced manufacturing. See OMB, "Efficient, Effective, Accountable." The Obama administration supported two significant expansions of federal funding: $175 million in competitive grant applications under the American Apprenticeship Program beginning in 2014, and the $90 million expansion of grant funding passed by Congress in fiscal year 2016. See Benjamin Collins, "Apprenticeship in the United States: Frequently Asked Questions," Congressional Research Service, January 29, 2016. In its final fiscal year 2017 budget proposal, the Obama administration outlined a series of ambitious Job Driven Training Proposals, including $2 billion to encourage state and local governments to increase employer participation in apprenticeships. See Department of Labor, "Budget in Brief Fiscal Year 2017," http://dol.gov/sites/default/files/documents/general/budget/FY2017BIB_0.pdf.

235. Bruce D. Meyer et al., "Household Surveys in Crisis," *Journal of Economic Perspectives* 29, no. 4 (Fall 2015), http://aeaweb.org/articles?id=10.1257/jep.29.4.199; Nicholas Eberstadt et. al, "'In Order That They Might Rest Their Arguments on Facts': The Vital Role of Government-Collected Data," Hamilton Project and American Enterprise Institute, March 2017, http://aei.org/wp-content/uploads/2017/03/THP_GovDataFacts_0317_Fixed.pdf.

236. Chopra and Gurwitz, "Modernizing America's Workforce Data Architecture"; Chopra, interview.

237. Goldie Blumenstyk, "Education Department Now Plans a College-Rating System Minus the Ratings," *Chronicle of Higher Education*, June 25, 2015, http://chronicle.com/article/Education-Department-Now-Plans/231137.

238. College Scorecard, U.S. Department of Education, http://collegescorecard.ed.gov.

239. See Andrew Kreighbaum, "Push for 'Unit Records' Revived," *Inside Higher Ed*, May 16, 2017, http://insidehighered.com/news/2017/05/16/bipartisan-bill-would-overturn-federal-ban-student-unit-record-database; Mel Leonor, "Could Senate Higher Ed Rewrite Expand Data Collection?" *Politico*, February 6, 2018, http://politico.com/newsletters/morning-education/2018/02/06/could-senate-higher-ed-rewrite-expand-data-collection-094318.

240. Chopra and Gurwitz, "Modernizing America's Workforce Data Architecture."

241. Elisa Rassen et al., *Using Labor Market Data to Improve Student Success* (Washington, DC: Aspen Institute, 2014), http://aspeninstitute.org/publications/using-labor-market-data-improve-student-success.

242. Emilie Rusch, "New Colorado Jobs Program Aims to Help Middle-Skill Workers Get Ahead," *Denver Post*, March 17, 2016, http://denverpost.com/2016/03/17/new-colorado-jobs-program-aims-to-help-middle-skill-workers-get-ahead.

243. *OECD Employment Outlook 2017*; World Trade Organization, *World Trade Report 2017: Trade, Technology and Jobs* (Geneva: World Trade Organization, 2017), http://wto.org/english/res_e/booksp_e/world_trade_report17_e.pdf.

244. Michael Trebilcock and Sally Wong, "Trade, Technology and Transitions: Trampolines or Safety Nets for Displaced Workers?" (unpublished manuscript).

245. Anne Sylvaine Chassany, "Emmanuel Macron Pushes Through French Labour Law Reforms," *Financial Times*, September 22, 2017, http://ft.com/content/a9ad1728-9f68-11e7-9a86-4d5a475ba4c5.

246. Niklas Engbom, Enrica Detragiache, and Faezeh Raei, "The German Labor Market Reforms and Post-Unemployment Earnings," IMF Working Paper 15/162, July 2015, http://imf.org/external/pubs/ft/wp/2015/wp15162.pdf.

247. National Skills Coalition, "Skills for Good Jobs: Agenda 2018," http://nationalskillscoalition.org/resources/publications/file/Skills-for-Good-Jobs-Agenda-2018.pdf.

248. Conor McKay, Ethan Pollack, and Alistair Fitzpayne, "Modernizing Unemployment Insurance for the Changing Nature of Work," Aspen Institute Future of Work Initiative, January 2018.

249. Alden and Litan, "A New Deal for the Twenty-First Century."

250. For a review of the large literature on wage insurance, evidence from other countries, and suggestions for greater testing of its effectiveness, see Stephen Wandner, "Wage Insurance as a Policy Option in the United States," Upjohn Institute Working Paper, January 17, 2016.

251. Mihir Desai, "Move Americans to Jobs, Not the Other Way Around," *Bloomberg View*, August 28, 2017, http://bloomberg.com/view/articles/2017-08-28/move-americans-to-jobs-not-the-other-way-around.

252. The Aspen Institute, "A Resource Guide for College/Career Navigators or Those Interested in Starting a Navigator Program," November 2014, http://aspenwsi.org/wordpress/wp-content/uploads/CareerNavigators.pdf.

253. Claire Cain Miller and Quoctrung Bui, "Switching Careers Doesn't Have to Be Hard: Charting Jobs That Are Similar to Your Own," *New York Times*, July 27, 2017, http://nytimes.com/2017/07/27/upshot/switching-careers-is-hard-it-doesnt-have-to-be.html.

254. Dick M. Carpenter II et al., *License to Work: A National Study of Burdens from Occupational Licensing*, 2nd ed. (Arlington, VA: Institute for Justice, 2017), http://ij.org/report/license-work-2.

255. Robert J. Thornton and Edward J. Timmons, "The De-licensing of Occupations in the United States," *Monthly Labor Review*, May 18, 2015, http://www.bls.gov/opub

/mlr/2015/article/the-de-licensing-of-occupations-in-the-united-states.htm.

256. National Conference of State Legislatures, *Occupational Licensing: Assessing State Policy and Practice* (Washington, DC: National Conference of State Legislatures, August 17, 2017), http://ncsl.org/portals/1/documents/labor/licensing/occupational_licensing.pdf.

257. "TechHire," Opportunity@Work, Inc, http://opportunityatwork.org/techhire.

258. Andy Stern et al., *Raising the Floor: How a Universal Basic Income Can Renew Our Economy and Rebuild the American Dream* (Philadelphia: PublicAffairs, 2016).

259. Charles Murray, *In Our Hands: A Plan to End the Welfare State* (Washington, DC: AEI Press, 2006).

260. "Realizing Human Potential in the Fourth Industrial Revolution: An Agenda for Leaders to Shape the Future of Education, Gender and Work," World Economic Forum, January 2017; *OECD 2017 Employment Outlook*.

261. Sebastian Schulze-Marmeling, "France: Occupational Personal Accounts Planned for 2017," EurWORK European Observatory of Working Life, November 30, 2015, http://eurofound.europa.eu/observatories/eurwork/articles/labour-market/france-occupational-personal-accounts-planned-for-2017.

262. Nick Hanauer and David Rolf, "Shared Security, Shared Growth," *Democracy Journal*, June 1, 2015, http://democracyjournal.org/magazine/37/shared-security-shared-growth.

263. David Rolf et al, "Portable Benefits in the 21st Century," Aspen Institute, 2016, http://assets.aspeninstitute.org/content/uploads/files/content/upload/Portable_Benefits_final.pdf.

264. Sarah Kessler, "US Legislators Just Proposed a $20-Million Experiment That Could Bring Benefits to Freelance and Gig-Economy Workers," *Quartz*, May 25, 2017, http://qz.com/991270/us-senator-mark-warner-proposed-a-20-million-fund-to-experiment-with-portable-benefits-for-freelancers-gig-economy-workers-and-contractors; Seth D. Harris and Alan B. Krueger, "A Proposal for Modernizing Labor Laws for Twenty-First Century Work: The 'Independent Worker,'" Hamilton Project, Brookings Institution, December 2015, http://brookings.edu/research/a-proposal-for-modernizing-labor-laws-for-21st-century-work-the-independent-worker.

265. "Why So Many Dutch People Work Part Time," *Economist*, May 12, 2015, http://economist.com/blogs/economist-explains/2015/05/economist-explains-12.

266. Rolf et al., "Portable Benefits."

267. Quinton, "With Growth of the Gig Economy."

268. Kyle James, "Nine Big Companies That Offer Benefits for Part-Time Workers," *Christian Science Monitor*, October 6, 2015, http://csmonitor.com/Business/Saving-Money/2015/1006/Nine-big-companies-that-offer-benefits-for-part-time-workers.

269. "Starbucks to Boost Pay, Benefits After U.S. Lowers Corporate Taxes," Reuters, January 24, 2018, http://reuters.com/article/us-starbucks-tax/starbucks-to-boost-pay-benefits-after-u-s-lowers-corporate-taxes-idUSKBN1FD1CD.

270. NGA Center for Best Practices, http://nga.org/cms/center; "U.S. Conference of Mayors

Business Council 2016 Best Practices Report," http://usmayors.org/wp-content /uploads/2017/03/bc2016.pdf.

271. Carnevale et al., *Good Jobs That Pay Without a BA.*

272. Glenn Marie-Lange, Quentin Wodon, and Kevin Carey, eds., *The Changing Wealth of Nations 2018: Building a Sustainable Future* (Washington, DC: World Bank, 2018), http://openknowledge.worldbank.org/handle/10986/29001.

273. "Baldrige Performance Excellence Program," National Institute of Standards and Technology, October 25, 2018, http://nist.gov/baldrige/how-baldrige-works/about -baldrige/baldrige-faqs.

274. John Holusha, "The Baldrige Badge of Courage—and Quality," *New York Times*, October 21, 1990, http://nytimes.com/1990/10/21/business/the-baldrige-badge-of -courage-and-quality.html.

275. HeroX, Tongal, XPrize, and MIT's Solve are all incentive challenge platforms designed to help organizations crowdsource problems and generate solutions through a competition. HeroX, Tongal, and XPrize all provide a monetary prize if the challenge generates a solution. See http://solve.mit.edu; http://www.herox.com; http://tongal .com; http://www.xprize.org.

276. On the priorities for the December 2018 G20 Summit, see "Overview of Argentina's G-20 Presidency 2018," http://g20.argentina.gob.ar/en /overview-argentinas-g20-presidency-2018.

ACRONYMS

AI
artificial intelligence

B Corp
benefit corporation

CDFI
community development
financial institution

CFPB
Consumer Financial Protection
Bureau

CRA
Community
Reinvestment Act

CTE
career and technical education

EITC
Earned Income Tax Credit

EZ
enterprise zone

FCC
Federal Communications
Commission

G20
Group of Twenty

GDP
gross domestic product

JSC
job security council

MGI
McKinsey Global Institute

NAFTA
North American
Free Trade Agreement

NGO
nongovernmental organization

NIST
National Institute of Standards
and Technology

OECD
Organization for Economic Cooperation and Development

PRO Neighborhoods
Partnerships for Raising Opportunity in Neighborhoods

R&D
research and development

SBIR
Small Business Innovation Research

SSDI
Social Security Disability Insurance

STEM
science, technology, engineering, and mathematics

TAA
Trade Adjustment Assistance

TPP
Trans-Pacific Partnership

UBI
universal basic income

UI
unemployment insurance

WIA
Workforce Investment Act

WIOA
Workforce Innovation and Opportunity Act

TASK FORCE MEMBERS

Task Force members are asked to join a consensus signifying that they endorse "the general policy thrust and judgments reached by the group, though not necessarily every finding and recommendation." They participate in the Task Force in their individual, not their institutional, capacities.

Chike Aguh serves as the CEO of EveryoneOn, a national nonprofit dedicated to closing the digital divide. The organization has to date connected over five hundred thousand low-income Americans in forty-eight states to the internet, computers, and digital skills, and aims to connect more than one million low-income people in total before the end of 2020. Previously, Aguh worked as an education policy official under New York City Mayor Michael Bloomberg, a second-grade teacher, a Teach For America corps member, a Fulbright scholar in Thailand, and a director of corporate strategy at the Advisory Board Company. He holds a BA from Tufts University, an EdM from the Harvard Graduate School of Education, an MPA from the Harvard Kennedy School, and an MBA from the University of Pennsylvania's Wharton School. He is a 2017 Presidential Leadership Scholar, term member at the Council on Foreign Relations (CFR), NationSwell Council member, former board president at Code in the Schools, and member of the Harvard Kennedy School's alumni board of directors.

Edward Alden is the Bernard L. Schwartz senior fellow at CFR, specializing in U.S. economic competitiveness. He is the author of the book *Failure to Adjust: How Americans Got Left Behind in the Global Economy*, which focuses on the federal government's failure to respond effectively to competitive challenges on issues such as trade, currency, worker retraining programs, education, and infrastructure. In addition, Alden is the director of the CFR Renewing America publication series and coauthor of the CFR discussion paper "A New Deal for the Twenty-First Century." Alden's previous book, *The Closing of the American Border: Terrorism, Immigration, and Security Since 9/11*, was a finalist for the Lukas Book Prize for narrative nonfiction in 2009. He was the project codirector of the 2011 CFR-sponsored Independent Task Force Report, *U.S. Trade and Investment Policy*, and the project director of the 2009 CFR-sponsored Independent Task Force Report, *U.S. Immigration Policy*. Alden was previously the Washington bureau chief for the *Financial Times* and prior to that the newspaper's Canada bureau chief, based in Toronto. He earned a master's degree in international relations from the University of California, Berkeley, and pursued doctoral studies before returning to a journalism career.

Eric R. Biel is senior advisor to the Fair Labor Association, a multistakeholder organization that brings together business, civil society organizations, and colleges and universities to improve working conditions globally through adherence to international labor standards. From 2012 to 2017, Biel served as associate deputy undersecretary in the U.S. Department of Labor's Bureau of International Labor Affairs (ILAB), where he led ILAB's work on a diverse set of issues. After leaving government, he worked on projects with business, law, and nonprofit groups and was a frequent speaker on trade, labor, and business and human rights issues. From 2000 to 2011, Biel held several positions outside government, including deputy Washington director and senior counsel at Human Rights First. His prior government service, from 1990 to 2000, included working in senior positions at the Department of Commerce, as executive director of the bipartisan Commission on Protecting and Reducing Government Secrecy, and as trade counsel for the Senate Finance Committee. Since 2008, Biel has taught a course at the Georgetown University Law Center, "Human Rights at the Intersection of Trade and Corporate Responsibility." He has a BA from Johns Hopkins University and a joint JD-MPA from Yale Law School and Princeton University's Woodrow Wilson School of Public and International Affairs.

Allen Blue is vice president of product management and cofounder of LinkedIn, the online professional network. He is responsible for LinkedIn's overall product strategy. He also sponsors LinkedIn's work and education products within the economic graph team, including the products and platforms supporting Skillful.com, a joint effort between LinkedIn and the Markle Foundation to close the middle-skills gap in the United States. He advises several start-ups in Silicon Valley, most of which are focused on improving health and education. He sat on the U.S. Commerce Department's Data Advisory Council, helping guide the department's efforts to make its data broadly available to American businesses. Blue serves on the boards of the Hope Street Group, a nonprofit that focuses on bringing economic opportunity to Americans through a combination of policy and practice, and Change.org, an online destination for making grassroots-driven change easier. Before LinkedIn, Blue cofounded SocialNet.com, an online dating service, and graduated from Stanford University.

John Engler is the interim president of Michigan State University, the former three-term governor of Michigan, and the former president of two of the most influential U.S. business associations, the National Association of Manufacturers and the Business Roundtable. Engler headed the Business Roundtable from 2011 to 2017, leading Washington's preeminent advocacy organization for economic growth, global competitiveness, and job creation. From 2004 to 2010, Engler served as president and CEO of the National Association of Manufacturers, the largest manufacturing association in the United States. Engler came to the trade association world following a distinguished career in Michigan politics. He served for twenty years in the Michigan legislature, including seven years as state Senate majority leader. Elected governor in 1990, he served as the state's forty-sixth governor from 1991 to 2003. Engler's fellow governors elected him to chair both the National Governors Association and the Republican Governors Association. In 2001, *Governing* magazine honored him among its Public Officials of the Year. Engler currently serves as an independent trustee for the Fidelity fixed income and asset allocation board and is on the board of directors for Universal Forest Products and K12 Inc. Previously, Engler served as a director of Delta Air Lines and Dow Jones & Company and as a trustee of the Munder Funds. Engler graduated from Michigan State University with a bachelor of science in agricultural economics and later earned a law degree from Western Michigan University's Cooley Law School.

Diana Farrell is the founding president and CEO of the JPMorgan Chase Institute, where she has created a legacy of producing and publishing unique data analyses and insights that leverage the bank's own transactions data. Previously, Farrell was the global head of the McKinsey Center for Government and the McKinsey Global Institute. Farrell served in the White House as deputy director of the National Economic Council and deputy assistant to the president on economic policy from 2009 to 2010. During her tenure, she led inter-agency processes and stakeholder management on a broad portfolio of economic and legislative initiatives. Farrell coordinated policy development and stakeholder engagement around the passage of the Dodd-Frank Act and served as a member of the Presidential Task Force on the Auto Industry. Farrell currently serves on the board of directors for eBay, the Urban Institute, Wesleyan University, and Washington International School. In addition, Farrell is a trustee of the Trilateral Commission and a member of CFR, the Economic Club of New York, and the Bretton Woods Committee. Farrell holds a BA from Wesleyan University, from which she was awarded a Distinguished Alumna award, and an MBA from Harvard Business School.

Kian Gohar, a futurist, entrepreneur, and innovation expert, helps inspire the world's largest companies to harness disruptive technology trends that will transform industry in the next decade and beyond. He is a master facilitator and has coached the C-suite of over forty companies in the Fortune 500 on topics as diverse as technology disruption, transformational innovation, exponential thinking, the future of work, crowdsourcing, the future of mobility, emerging markets, and leadership. Gohar is founder of the world's leading ecosystem for corporate innovation, the Innovation Partnership Program—a joint venture of the XPRIZE Foundation and Singularity University—and Geolab, an innovation advisory lab. His twenty-year innovation career spans venture capital, academia, and startups around the world. A sought-after public speaker, he has presented on the future of work at the World Economic Forum and been featured on CNBC. Gohar speaks five languages, was a Luce scholar in China, and is a graduate of Harvard Business School, the London School of Economics, and Northwestern University.

Gordon Hanson holds the Pacific economic cooperation chair in international economic relations at the University of California (UC), San Diego, and has faculty positions in the university's Department of Economics and School of Global Policy and Strategy, where he also is director of the Center on Global Transformation. He is a research associate at the National Bureau of Economic Research, a member of CFR, and coeditor of the *Journal of Economic Perspectives*. He is a past coeditor of the *Review of Economics and Statistics* and the *Journal of Development Economics*. Prior to joining UC-San Diego in 2001, he served on the economics faculty of the University of Michigan and the University of Texas. Hanson specializes in the economics of international trade, international migration, and foreign direct investment. He has published extensively in the top academic journals of the economics discipline, is widely cited for his research by scholars from across the social sciences, and is frequently quoted in major media outlets. Hanson's current research addresses how trade with China has affected the U.S. labor market, the consequences of low- and high-skilled immigration for the U.S. economy, and the long-run determinants of comparative advantage. Hanson received his BA from Occidental College and his PhD from the Massachusetts Institute of Technology.

Robert M. Kimmitt is currently the senior international counsel at WilmerHale. He has held a variety of senior positions in government and the private sector at the intersection of international business, finance, law, and policy. From 2005 to 2009, he served as deputy secretary of the treasury. Earlier, he was U.S. ambassador to Germany, undersecretary of state for political affairs, general counsel to the U.S. Treasury Department, and executive secretary and general counsel of the National Security Council at the White House. In addition to his government service, Kimmitt was executive vice president for global public policy at Time Warner and vice chairman and president of Commerce One. Kimmitt graduated with distinction from the U.S. Military Academy at West Point in 1969, served in combat with the

173rd Airborne Brigade in Vietnam, and retired as a major general in the Army Reserve. He received his law degree from Georgetown University in 1977. Kimmitt is a member of the supervisory board of Lufthansa AG, the international advisory boards of Allianz SE and the Maureen and Mike Mansfield Foundation, the global advisory board of Tokai Tokyo Financial Holdings, and the boards of the Arthur F. Burns Fellowship, the Atlantic Council, USA Rugby, and the Vietnam Veterans Memorial Fund. He is a member of the American Academy of Diplomacy, CFR, and the Trilateral Commission and chairman emeritus of the American Council on Germany.

Susan Lund is a partner at McKinsey & Company and a leader of the McKinsey Global Institute. As an economist, she researches the impact of technology on labor markets, finance, and globalization. Her most recent research modeled the impact of automation and artificial intelligence on the future of work and the workforce. Other recent reports measured the size of the independent workforce in the United States and Europe, assessed the potential economic impact of digital finance and mobile money in developing countries, and examined how globalization is evolving in the digital era. Lund frequently discusses research findings with CEOs and other executives at global Fortune 500 companies and speaks at global conferences. She has authored numerous articles in leading business publications, including the *Harvard Business Review*, the *Financial Times*, the *Wall Street Journal*, the *Washington Post*, and *Foreign Affairs*. Lund is on the board of directors of the National Association for Business Economics and is a member of CFR, the Bretton Woods Committee, and the Conference of Business Economists. She holds a BA from Northwestern University and a PhD from Stanford University.

Jack Markell served from 2009 to 2017 as the governor of Delaware. During his tenure, Markell led significant investments in improved early childhood education, language immersion programs, heightened college access for low-income students, and some of the most aggressive workforce development efforts in the country. Markell was selected by his peers to serve as chair of both the Democratic Governors Association and the bipartisan National Governors Association. Previously, Markell served as Delaware's state treasurer. Prior to public service, Markell helped lead the wireless technology revolution as the thirteenth employee at Nextel (a name he coined), where he served as senior vice president for corporate development. He also worked at

Comcast Corporation and McKinsey & Company. Markell serves on the national board of directors of Jobs for America's Graduates and Upstream USA and is a trustee of the Annie E. Casey Foundation. He holds a BA from Brown University and an MBA from the University of Chicago. Markell is a Henry Crown fellow and a Rodel fellow, both at the Aspen Institute.

Jamie P. Merisotis is a globally recognized leader in philanthropy, education, and public policy. Since 2008, he has served as president and CEO of Lumina Foundation, an independent, private foundation that is committed to making opportunities for learning beyond high school available to all. His work includes extensive global experience as an advisor and consultant in southern Africa, the former Soviet Union, Europe, and other parts of the world. He previously served as CEO of the Institute for Higher Education Policy in Washington, DC, and as executive director of a national commission on college affordability appointed by the U.S. president and congressional leaders. Merisotis is the author of the widely acclaimed book *America Needs Talent*, listed among *Booklist*'s "Top 10 Business Books: 2016." A frequent media commentator and contributor, Merisotis has written for the *Washington Post, New York Times, Wall Street Journal, Stanford Social Innovation Review, Washington Monthly, Huffington Post, Politico*, and other publications. He is a member of CFR and serves as a trustee for a diverse array of organizations around the world, including the Children's Museum of Indianapolis, which he chairs; Bates College in Maine; the Council on Foundations in Washington, DC; and Anatolia College in Greece.

Rodrick T. Miller is an economic development leader known for his ability to maneuver in complex political and business environments and craft strategies and structure deals that provide long-term value to communities and investors. He is the president and CEO of Ascendant Global, a boutique economic development firm established in early 2017. Ascendant focuses on providing bold growth solutions to help economies sustain themselves and gain jobs and private investment. Previously, Miller was president and CEO of the Detroit Economic Growth Corporation (DEGC), the public-private partnership charged with leading the economic revitalization of Detroit. Under Miller's leadership, the DEGC brought more than $1 billion in new investments and twelve thousand new jobs to Detroit. Prior to joining the DEGC, Miller was the president of the New Orleans Business Alliance, where he focused the organization's efforts on lowering barriers to entry in the marketplace, increasing transparency, and driving inclusive economic growth. Miller holds a bachelor of science in international business from Saint Augustine's University, a graduate diploma in finance that he earned in Mexico as a Fulbright fellow, and a master of public policy from Harvard University. He is a term member of CFR and a board member of Priority Health Insurance, the International Economic Development Council, and the Federal Reserve Board's Community Advisory Council.

Eduardo J. Padrón is the president of Miami Dade College, a national model of student achievement and the largest institution of higher education in the United States. In 2016, President Barack Obama awarded him the Presidential Medal of Freedom, the highest civilian honor in the United States, for being a prominent national voice for access and inclusion in higher education. In 2009, *Time* magazine included him among the "10 Best College Presidents" in the United States; in 2010, *Florida Trend* magazine named him "Floridian of the Year"; and in 2011, the *Washington Post* recognized him as one of the eight most influential college presidents nationwide. He is a recipient of the Carnegie Corporation's Centennial Academic Leadership Award, the Citizen Service Award from Voices for National Service, and the TIAA Institute's Hesburgh Award, the highest honor in U.S. higher education. He is also a U.S. News STEM Leadership Hall of Fame inductee and an Ascend fellow at the Aspen Institute. Six American presidents have selected him to serve on posts of national prominence. He serves on the boards of CFR, the Urban Institute, and the International Association of University Presidents. He is the past chairman of the Business-Higher Education Forum, the American Council on Education, and the Association of American Colleges and Universities.

Penny Pritzker is the founder and chairman of PSP Partners and its affiliates, Pritzker Realty Group, PSP Capital, and PSP Growth. From 2013 through 2017, she served as U.S. secretary of commerce in the Barack Obama administration. Pritzker is an entrepreneur, civic leader, and philanthropist with more than twenty-five years of experience in numerous industries. She founded Vi Senior Living (formerly known as Classic Residence by Hyatt) and cofounded the Parking Spot, Artemis Real Estate Partners, and Skills for America's Future. She is the former chairman of the board of TransUnion and is a past board member of Hyatt Hotels Corporation, the Wrigley Company, Marmon Group, LaSalle Bank Corporation, and CFR. Pritzker is also a member of the boards of Microsoft and the Carnegie Endowment for International Peace, a member of the Aspen Strategy Group and the Aspen Economic Strategy Group, and a co-chair of the Cyber Readiness Institute. She was also a member of the board of trustees of Stanford University and the Harvard University board of overseers. Pritzker also served on President Obama's Council on Jobs and Competitiveness and his Economic Recovery Advisory Board. Pritzker earned a BA in economics from Harvard University and a JD and MBA from Stanford University. Pritzker and her husband, Dr. Bryan Traubert, cofounded the Pritzker Traubert Foundation, a private philanthropic foundation that works to foster increased economic opportunity for Chicago's families.

Cecilia E. Rouse is the dean of Princeton University's Woodrow Wilson School of Public and International Affairs and the Lawrence and Shirley Katzman and Lewis and Anna Ernst professor in the economics of education. She is the founding director of Princeton University's Education Research Section and is a member of the National Academy of Education. Her primary research interests are in labor economics, with a focus on the economics of education. Rouse has served as an editor of the *Journal of Labor Economics* and is currently a senior editor of the *Future of Children*. From 1998 to 1999 she served in the White House on the National Economic Council, and from 2009 to 2011 served as a member of the president's Council of Economic Advisers. She is a member of the board of directors of the National Bureau of Economic Research and MDRC, and is a director of the T. Rowe Price equity mutual funds and fixed income mutual funds. She received her BA and PhD in economics from Harvard University.

Lee J. Styslinger III is the chairman and CEO of Altec Inc., the holding company for Altec Industries, Capital Services, National Equipment Company, Altec Worldwide, Global Rental, and Altec Ventures. He became president of Altec in 1994 and was named CEO in 1997. Altec was founded in 1929 by his grandfather and today is a global leader that designs and manufactures products and services for the electric utility, telecommunications, and contractor markets in over one hundred countries throughout the world. Styslinger serves on the boards of Regions Financial Corporation, Vulcan Materials Company, Workday, Harvard Business School, Children's Hospital of Alabama, and the Altec/Styslinger Foundation. He is also a member of the Business Roundtable, the Business Council, and CFR. Styslinger was appointed to the President's Export Council by President George W. Bush, where he served from 2006 to 2008, advising the president on trade policy. In 2017, he served on President Donald J. Trump's manufacturing council. Styslinger earned his BA from Northwestern University and his MBA from Harvard University.

Hemant Taneja is a managing director at General Catalyst Partners. He joined the firm in 2002 and launched its Silicon Valley office in 2011. Taneja invests in founders with authentic missions that have the potential to change entire industries. His investment thesis, known as "economies of unscale," describes the belief that small, tightly focused companies can leverage web services, data sets, and artificial intelligence to successfully launch and compete against much larger, more established competitors. His book, *Unscaled: How AI and a New Generation of Upstarts Are Creating the Economy of the Future*, explores this thesis in depth, and was published in 2018. Taneja's current investment portfolio ranges across the fields of medicine, finance, and education, including companies such as Stripe, Snapchat, Color Genomics, Gusto, Livongo Health, TuneIn, ClassDojo, Fundbox, Digit, Grammarly, and Fractyl. Alongside his venture work, he cofounded Advanced Energy Economy, a public policy advocacy group focused on advanced energy solutions, and has served on the board of directors of the nonprofit education organization Khan Academy. He has also been a lecturer at the Massachusetts Institute of Technology (MIT) and Stanford University. Taneja holds five degrees from MIT.

Laura Taylor-Kale most recently served as the deputy assistant secretary for manufacturing at the U.S. Department of Commerce. In this position, she oversaw a broad portfolio of programs and trade policies aimed at increasing global opportunities and the international competitiveness of U.S. manufacturers. Taylor-Kale also served as the senior advisor for policy and operations at the Overseas Private Investment Corporation (OPIC), where she coordinated policy for OPIC's $5 billion portfolio of investments in sub-Saharan Africa and Asia. She has also held positions at the World Bank as an advisor to the U.S. executive director and the vice president for sustainable development. From 2003 to 2012, Taylor-Kale was a foreign service officer in the U.S. Department of State, in which capacity she was posted to Afghanistan, India, Ivory Coast, and the Bureau of Economic and Business Affairs. She holds a BA in economics and anthropology from Smith College, an MPA from Princeton University's Woodrow Wilson School of Public and International Affairs, and an MBA from New York University's Stern School of Business. As an international affairs fellow at CFR, she is researching the impact of artificial intelligence on U.S. economic competitiveness and the future of manufacturing.

TASK FORCE OBSERVERS

Observers participate in Task Force discussions but are not asked to join the consensus. They participate in their individual, not their institutional, capacities.

Heidi Crebo-Rediker is an adjunct senior fellow at CFR and the CEO of International Capital Strategies. Prior to this, she served as the State Department's first chief economist. Appointed by then Secretary of State Hillary Rodham Clinton as a centerpiece of her "economic statecraft" initiative, Crebo-Rediker provided advice and analysis to the secretary on foreign policy issues with a significant economic or financial component. Prior to this, Crebo-Rediker was the chief of international finance and economics for the Senate Committee on Foreign Relations, following nearly two decades in Europe as a senior investment banker. During her time in the Senate, she was the architect of the bipartisan National Infrastructure Bank legislation (BUILD Act), introduced in March 2011 and included in President Barack Obama's Jumpstart Our Business Startups (JOBS) Act. Over her investment banking career, she managed businesses ranging from European and emerging-markets debt capital markets to sovereign, supranational, and public-sector banking. In this capacity, she managed public and private financings for governments, corporations, and banks, and performed related advisory work. On returning to Washington, DC, she was the founding codirector of the Global Strategic Finance Initiative at the New America Foundation. Crebo-Rediker was named one of the top twenty-five women in business by the *Wall Street Journal Europe*. She holds degrees from Dartmouth College and the London School of Economics.

Kyla Griffith is the chief of staff to founder and chairman Penny Pritzker at PSP Partners. Griffith is responsible for developing and executing the chairman's strategic goals across her business, civic, and philanthropic engagements. A seven-year veteran of the Obama administration, Griffith served as special advisor to the secretary and director of the immediate office of the secretary at the U.S. Department of Commerce. Griffith managed the daily flow of people, paper, and information to the secretary and served as liaison to department leadership, policy experts, and business leaders across the globe. Griffith traveled with Secretary Pritzker to twenty countries and over fifty U.S. cities, advocating on behalf of American companies and workers. Before joining the Commerce Department, Griffith worked in the office of the White House counsel, specializing in ethics, compliance, and political law. She began her White House tenure in the Domestic Policy Council, conducting policy research and engaging stakeholders on economic opportunity and social mobility issues. Previously, Griffith worked at Gunderson Dettmer, the leading business law firm for entrepreneurs and emerging growth companies. Griffith graduated from Boston University's dual-degree program in 2008 with a bachelor of arts in political science and a bachelor of science in communication.

Jim Hock serves as senior vice president at PSP Partners, a private investment firm that takes a long-term, fundamental approach to investing and building businesses in real estate, private businesses, and funds and partnership opportunities. Previously, Hock served in the Obama administration as chief of staff to Secretary of Commerce Penny Pritzker at the U.S. Department of Commerce, where they created the first department initiative on skilled workforce training. Hock also served for more than a year as senior advisor and director of public affairs at the department. In these roles, Hock was instrumental in the management of the agency, creating and framing its Open for Business Agenda and serving as the department's liaison to the White House and other federal agencies and stakeholders. Prior to his service in the administration, Hock founded 463 Communications (now Vrge), a communications agency for technology and clean energy firms within the Next 15 family of companies. As partner at 463, Hock worked with some of the premier U.S. brands in technology on business strategy, policy, communications, digital media, and marketing. Before launching 463, Hock served as spokesman and advisor to U.S. Senator Dianne Feinstein. In addition, Hock worked as a high school teacher and a Jesuit volunteer for at-risk youth in East Los Angeles, and is the author of *Hollywood's Team*, a book about his father and his Los Angeles Rams team of the 1950s. Hock has a BA from Fordham University and an MA in public policy from Georgetown University.

Dane Linn is a vice president for the Business Roundtable (BRT). In this role, he oversees the education and workforce committee and the immigration committee, advancing the BRT's positions on education reform, immigration reform, U.S. innovation capacity, and workforce preparedness. Linn joined the BRT most recently from the College Board, where he served as executive director of state policy. Prior to the College Board, Linn served as director of the educational policy division of the National Governors Association (NGA) Center for Best Practices. During his sixteen years in this role, Linn represented governors' education policy issues at the federal level and to state and local associations. He also co-led the development of the Common Core State Standards, which have been adopted by forty-six states. In addition, Linn has led national efforts to ensure that more students are college- and career-ready and worked on issues related to science, technology, engineering, and mathematics (STEM), early childhood, the Perkins Act and the Workforce Investment Act, and high school redesign. Before joining the NGA, Linn worked for fourteen years in the education system as coordinator of the Office of Special Education Programs for the West Virginia Department of Education, principal of Guyan Valley Elementary School in West Virginia, and teacher and then assistant principal at Matheny Grade School in West Virginia. Linn holds a bachelor's degree in elementary education and special education from Cabrini College and a master's degree in education administration from West Virginia Graduate College, and is a doctoral candidate at Virginia Polytechnic Institute.

Robert E. Litan is a nonresident senior fellow at the Brookings Institution. As both an attorney and economist, Litan has held numerous positions in the private, nonprofit, and government sectors during his forty-year career, including director of economic studies at the Brookings Institution and positions at the Kauffman Foundation and Bloomberg Government. He has authored or coauthored twenty-six books and over two hundred articles on economic policy in professional journals and magazines.

Anya Schmemann (ex officio) is Washington director of Global Communications and Outreach and director of the Independent Task

Force Program at CFR in Washington, DC. She recently served as assistant dean for communications and outreach at American University's School of International Service. At CFR, Schmemann has overseen over thirteen high-level Task Forces on topics including Arctic strategy, nuclear weapons, climate change, immigration, trade policy, and internet governance, and on U.S. policy toward Afghanistan, Brazil, North Korea, Pakistan, and Turkey. Schmemann previously managed communications at the Harvard Kennedy School's Belfer Center for Science and International Affairs and administered the Caspian Studies Program there. She coordinated a research project on Russian security issues at the EastWest Institute in New York and was assistant director of CFR's Center for Preventive Action in New York, focusing on the Balkans and Central Asia. Schmemann received a BA in government and an MA in Russian, East European, and Central Asian Studies, both from Harvard University. She was a Truman national security fellow and a nonresident senior fellow at the Center for the National Interest, and is a life member of CFR.

Michael Spence is a distinguished visiting fellow at CFR. Previously, Spence served as chairman of the independent Commission on Growth and Development. He continues to serve as a senior fellow at Stanford University's Hoover Institution and as a professor of economics at New York University. After teaching at Stanford and Harvard Universities, he served as dean of the Faculty of Arts and Sciences at Harvard from 1984 to 1990, and then dean of the Stanford Graduate School of Business from 1990 to 1999. Spence wrote the book *The Next Convergence: The Future of Economic Growth in a Multi-speed World*, and writes monthly commentary for *Project Syndicate* and occasional op-ed pieces in the *Financial Times* and other major media outlets. Spence is a recipient of the John Kenneth Galbraith prize for excellence in teaching and the John Bates Clark Medal, awarded to an economist under the age of forty for a "significant contribution to economic thought and knowledge." In 2001, Spence received the Nobel Prize in Economic Sciences. He earned his BA in philosophy at Princeton University and was selected for a Rhodes scholarship. He has a BS-MA in mathematics from Oxford University and received his PhD in economics at Harvard University. Spence has served on the boards of Genpact and MercadoLibre, and a number of private companies. He is a former member of the board of the Stanford Management Company. He is a senior adviser to Oak Hill Investment Management and a consultant to PIMCO.

Contributing CFR Staff

Maria Teresa Alzuru
Product Manager,
Product and Design

Patricia Lee Dorff
Editorial Director, Publishing

Shelton Fitch
Research Associate,
U.S. Competitiveness
and Foreign Policy

Julie Hersh
Production Editor, Publishing

Oliva McCoy
Interdepartmental
Program Assistant

Cayla Merrill
Graphic Designer,
Product and Design

Lisa Ortiz
Director, Product and Design

Anya Schmemann
Director,
Independent Task Force Program

Chelie Setzer
Program Coordinator,
Independent Task Force Program

Amanda Shendruk
Data Visualization Designer,
Product and Design

Contributing Volunteer Interns

Jonathan Coutinho
Geoeconomic Studies

Blake Ledna
Independent Task Force Program

Maureen McGinn
Geoeconomic Studies

Ellen Myers
Independent Task Force Program